AF564605

RESEARCH IN FINANCE
Corporate, Behavioral, Microfinance and E-finance Models

RESEARCH IN FINANCE

Corporate, Behavioral, Microfinance and E-finance Models

Edited by
ABDUL RAHMAN
and
ASHU BHOJWANI

REGAL PUBLICATIONS
New Delhi-110027

RESEARCH IN FINANCE

ISBN 978-81-8484-286-9

Type. by
S.S. COMPOSERS
3190, Mohindra Park, Shakur Basti, Delhi-110034.

Printed in India at
MAYUR ENTERPRISES
WZ Plot No. 3, Gujjar Market, Tihar Village, New Delhi-110018.

Published by
REGAL PUBLICATIONS
F-159, Rajouri Garden, New Delhi-110027.
Phone: +91-11-45546396
E-mail: regalbookspub@yahoo.com

Contents

Preface

Finance is receiving utmost attention from different corners. This proves that, this discipline has thoroughly entered the public domain. To bear out the strength of curiosity among academics and corporate professionals, large number of conferences throughout the world are devoted to this discipline. Hence, contributions to these discussions may be drawn from a variety of sub-themes of finance, including Corporate Finance, Behavioral Finance, Microfinance, and Electronic Finance.

The objective of this book is to offer students of commerce and management and practitioners of finance a series of 'cutting edge reviews of key topics in the area'. The current volume is based primarily—but not exclusively—on various models of finance. The contributors, who for the most part have engaged themselves as finance or management experts in management institutes, or doctoral scholars, have each set out to review the observations and supporting evidence from the literature on their particular topic. In its coverage the book might be considered as a unique one compared to other texts in the main or sub-themes of finance. The book in its way of presentation is a complementary to Keasey K., Thompson S., and Wright M. (eds.), Corporate Governance (Oxford, 1997), and Imam A., Rahman A., and Bhargava A., (eds.), Finance and Sustainable Development (Regal, 2012).

In compiling this book we would firstly like to thank our co-authors for the timeliness and quality of their contributions which made our editorial task manageable. Authors of individual chapters make their own thanks to those who have provided comments on earlier drafts. Dr. Mohammed Ashraf Ali, Associate Professor, Aligarh Muslim University and Dr. Rosy Karla, Assistant Professor, Amity Business School are acknowledged with thanks for their valuable suggestions, as is N.M. Leepsa and Sashikanta Tripathy for supporting us by sparing their valuable time in compilation of papers. We would also like to thank R.D.S. Bhatia of Regal Publications for his encouragement, support, and forbearance throughout the project.

ABDUL RAHMAN
ASHU BHOJWANI

Contributors

Abdul R[illegible]
N[illegible]

Ashu Bhojwani
[illegible]

Atul Shi[illegible]
[illegible]

Dr. Fulbagh [illegible]
[illegible]
Amritsar

B. Hari Babu
Manag[illegible]

N. M. Z[illegible]
[illegible]

Dr. Manish [illegible]
Institute [illegible]
Vidy[illegible]

Dr. Manoj Kumar [illegible]
[illegible]

Minaketan [illegible]
New [illegible]

Monica Sethi
Commerce [illegible]

Nandita M[illegible]

Om Prakash
[illegible]

Raghu [illegible]
[illegible]
of [illegible]

List of Contributors

Abdul Rahman is a Doctoral Scholar in the Vinod Gupta School of Management at the Indian Institute of Technology of Kharagpur.

Ashu Bhojwani is a Doctoral Scholar in the Department of Commerce and Managemet at Devi Ahilya Vishwa Vidyalaya of Indore.

Atul Shiva is an Assistant Professor at the Sri Aurobindo College of Commerce and Management of Ludhiana.

Dr. Fulbagh Singh is a Professor in the Department of Commerce and Business Management at the Gurunanak Dev University of Amritsar.

B. Hari Babu is an Assistant Professor in the Department of Business Management at the V.R. Siddhartha Engineering College of Vijayawada.

N.M. Leepsa is a Doctoral Scholar in the Vinod Gupta School of Management at the Indian Institute of Technology of Kharagpur.

Dr. Manish Sitlani is an Associate Professor in the International Institute of Professional Studies at the Devi Ahilya Vishwa Vidyalaya of Indore.

Dr. Manoj Kumar is an Associate Professor in the Department of Business Studies at the Lal Bahadur Shastri Institute of Management and Development Studies of Lucknow.

Minaketan Dash is a Trainee Project Manager at Thompson Digitals of New Delhi.

Monica Sethi is an Assistant Professor at the Sri Aurobindo College of Commerce and Management of Ludhiana.

Nandita Majumdar is a Freelance Researcher in Finance of Toronto.

Om Prakash is an Assistant Professor in the Department of Commerce at the Ramjas College of New Delhi.

Raghu Katragadda is an Assistant Professor in the Department of Business Management at the V.R. Siddhartha Engineering College of Vijayawada.

Prof. Ray Titus is a Chairperson and Professor at the Alliance Business School of Bangalore.

Renu Gupta is an Assistant Professor in the Department of Commerce at the University of Delhi of New Delhi.

Roshni Mohanty is a Doctoral Scholar in the Department of Commerce and Management at the Utkal University of Bhubaneswar.

Dr. Sajjan Mathew is trainer and consultant at the Alliance Business School of Bangalore.

Sasikantha Tripathy is a Doctoral Scholar in the Vinod Gupta School of Management at the Indian Institute of Technology of Kharagpur.

Shalini Srivastava is an Assistant Professor at the Accman Institute of Management of Noida.

Sree Vidya is a Doctoral Scholar in the Department of Anthropology at the Sri Venkateswara University of Tirupathi.

Dr. Sukhwinder Kaur is an Assistant Professor at the Hindu Kanya College of Kapurthala.

Prof. B.K. Surya Prakasa Rao is a Professor and Head in the Department of Management Sciences at the RVR & JC College of Engineering of Guntur.

1

Introduction: The Discipline of Finance—Some Competing Models

Abdul Rahman and Ashu Bhojwani

Money was never a big motivation for me, except as a way to keep score. The real excitement is playing the game.

—*Donald Trump*

Capital as such is not evil; it is its wrong use that is evil. Capital in some form or other will always be needed.

—*Mahatma Gandhi*

I. INTRODUCTION

Finance is a branch of economics concerned with resource allocation as well as resource management, acquisition and investment. Simply, finance is the study of how investors allocate their assets over time under the conditions of certainty and uncertainty. Moreover, every firm, whether big or small, needs finance to carry on its operations and to achieve its targets. Currently, finance is so requisite today that it can be called as the lifeblood of a firm.

Finance has been classified into two classes: (i) Public Finance; and (ii) Private Finance. Public finance deals with the provision, custody, and disbursement of the resources needed for the conduct of public or governmental functions. Private finance is concerned with requirements, receipts and disbursements of funds in case of an individual, a profit seeking business organization and a non-profit organization. Further, Private finance can be classified into: (i) Personal finance; (ii) Corporate finance; and (iii) Finance of non-profit organization.

Personal finance deals with the analysis of the principles and practices involved in managing one's own daily need of funds. The study of principles, practices, procedures, and problems concerning the financial management of profit making organizations engaged in the field of industry, trade, and commerce is undertaken under the discipline of corporate finance. A non-profit organization's primary goal is not to increase shareholder value; rather it is to provide some socially desirable need on an ongoing basis.

Apart from the classification made above, the discipline of finance consists of behavioral finance, microfinance and E-finance. Behavioral finance is the study of the influence of psychology on the behavior of financial practitioners and the subsequent effect on markets. The provision of banking services by poverty-focused financial institutions to poor parts of the population that are not being served by mainstream financial service providers can be termed as microfinance. The provision of financial services and markets using electronic communication and computation is E-finance.

In this chapter we take the view that to make sense of the finance debate it is necessary to consider the principal analytical background or approaches from which the journey begins. This is so because, as will be seen, much of the extensive discussion in the literature on the effectiveness of financial disciplines takes place without agreement on how these disciplines are modeled.

Corporate Finance Model

The problem of the corporate finance model has many aspects. It begins with a resemblance to the common actuarial problem of differentiating between specification, parameter, and process risks. Specification risk relates to the model structure and the selected probability distributions. Parameter risk assume the specification and the distributional parameters to be correct. Lastly, process risk assumes everything else as correct.

In financial modeling, there are many of these 'risks', and the model designer should be aware of them. The model designer must soar many barriers while formulating a corporate finance model. The risks might include functional mis-specification of the model, errors in risk and process identification, and failure of the accounting framework to adequately make known the figures needed for decision-making.

Cornell and Shapiro (1987), attempted to focus on two-folds, one by suggesting several ways in which the inclusion of additional stakeholders leads to new interpretations of classic problems in finance, and two by focusing on the distinction between explicit contractual claims that firms issue to non-investor stakeholders and also on implicit claims. They found that, the prices of implicit claims fall and stakeholders may even require that tacit understandings be replaced by explicit contracts. Dermiguc and Levine (1996), attempted to analyze the role of stock markets in corporate financing decisions and economic development, and presented new information on the co-development of financial intermediaries and stock markets. Their suggestion in the conclusion says that, policy-makers should not push stock market development, but they should remove impediments to stock markets, such as tax, legal, and regulatory barriers. Graham and Harvey (2001), surveyed about the cost of capital, capital budgeting and capital structure. They found that, large firms rely heavily on present value techniques and CAPM, while small firms are relatively likely to use the payback criterion. Also firms are concerned about financial flexibility and credit ratings when issuing debt, and EPS dilution. Their study found support for the pecking-order and trade-off capital structure hypotheses. Heaton (2002) explored the implications of a single specification of managerial irrationality in a simple model of corporate finance. He has focused on managerial optimism and its relation to the benefits and costs of free cash flow. He observed that, two dominant features emerge from the simple model with excessively optimistic managers and efficient capital markets. He disclosed that, his results imply underinvestment-overinvestment tradeoff related to free cash flow, without invoking asymmetric information or agency theory costs.

The corporate finance model as given by Affan (2008) consists of the following mentioned different types of models:

1. Corporate Model

This model is built for a company, which has a history and it is assumed to last forever (although that would not be in reality). The valuation of an enterprise begins with a historical analysis and some assumptions of terminal value are included in the model, because the cash flows are not projected forever.

2. Project Finance Model

This model is built for new projects, which has no history. These models focus on cash flows, Internal Rate of Return (IRR) and Payback of the project and are generally lifetime based.

3. Leveraged Buy Out Model (LBO)

A Leveraged Buy Out is a method under which a company is acquired by a person or an entity using the value of the company's assets to finance its acquisition; this allows for the acquirer or minimizes its cash outlay in making the purchase. The transaction is defined by an entry price, the holding period and exit price and the return earned by the equity investors. This model is based on the corporate model.

4. *Merger and Acquisition Model (M&A)*

Merger and Acquisition is an aspect of corporate strategy dealing with the buying, selling, dividing and combining different companies and similar entities that can help an enterprise grow rapidly in its sector or location or origin. The model explains the computation of earnings per share and other financial ratios before and after an acquisition. This model considers the specific synergies and cost savings generated by the transaction. This model is also based on the corporate model.

Behavioral Finance Model

Behavioral finance is a framework that augments some parts of standard finance and replaces other parts. It describes the behavior of investors and managers; it describes the outcomes of interactions between investors and managers in financial and capital markets; and it prescribes more effective behavior for investors and managers.

Standard finance is the body of knowledge built on the pillars of the arbitrage principles of Miller and Modigliani, the portfolio principles of Markowitz, the capital asset pricing theory of Sharpe, Lintner and Black, and the option-pricing theory of Black, Scholes and Merton. Standard finance is compelling because it uses a minimum of tools to build a unified theory, intended to answer all questions of finance. In contrast to this, behavioral finance is constructed with a few tools that have many uses. Some of the tools of behavioral finance are similar to those of standard finance, but some are different because they reflect a different model of human behavior.

Shefrin (1999), attempted to address two key behavioral impediments to the process of value maximization, one internal to the firm and the other external. He also explained the behavioral obstacles to value creation that are external to the firm. The behavioral characteristics of decision-making which are more prominent are presented in this paper. He found that internal destruction to behavior stems from psychologically induced errors made by managers and employees and external obstructions from errors made by analysts and investors. Ritter (2003) explains that, behavioral finance drops the traditional assumptions of expected utility maximization with rational investors in efficient markets. He attempts to disclose two building blocks of behavioral finance; one is cognitive psychology and the other limits to arbitrage. He concluded by saying that, behavioral finance is in its infancy and it is not a separate discipline, but instead will increasingly be part of mainstream finance. Fairchild (2004), attempted to focus on the effects of managerial irrationality in capital budgeting. He developed a principal-agent model which provides the basis for an experiment to test for behavioral factors. He developed a number of testable hypotheses. To test the hypotheses from the model he has outlined a possible experimental set-up. Mankert (2006) analyzed the Black-Litterman model by using two approaches; a mathematical and a behavioral finance approach. She derived the BL model mathematically using a sampling theoretical approach. Further, she has drawn implications from research results within the behavioral finance indicating that, portfolio output given by BL model appears more intuitive to fund managers than portfolios generated by the Markowitz model. Statman (2008), attempted to differentiate behavioral finance with standard finance by saying that, behavioral finance is a framework that augments some parts of standard finance and replaces other parts. He also explains difference between rational investors and normal investors. A close look at the behavioral portfolio theory has been made in this study. He along with Shefrin developed a model moving a little bit from Capital Asset Pricing Model to Behavioral Asset Pricing Model (BAPM). Iyengar and Chun (2010) proposed a model for jointly predicting stock price and volume at the tick-by-tick level. They modeled investors' preferences by a random utility model that incorporates several important behavioral biases. Their model is a logistic regression model and resorted to Morkov Chain Monte Carlo method to estimate the model parameters. Their goal of developing this model is to predict the market impact function and volume-weighted average price of individual stocks. Ramesh and Venkateshwarulu (2011) made an attempt to model the prediction of asset prices based on both the market data and the behavior of the market participants. Further, the behavior of the market participants has been modeled in present quantitative behavioral approach. They applied the methodology to gold asset class to validate the present method. Finally, after rigorous testing of the model they indicated that, the model presented is better in predicting the financial asset prices over the conventional mathematical models.

The below mentioned are some of the proposed models for behavioral finance.

1. Quantitative Behavioral Model

This is a new discipline that uses mathematical and statistical methodology to understand behavioral biases in conjunction with valuation. This model is a blend of the quantitative techniques used for financial prediction and the behavior of the market participants who use these techniques to predict the financial asset prices. This model predicts the number of participants in each category, for most of the times the market does not contain theses facts. The model observes these participants and finally after observation a conclusion can be drawn that the behavior of the participants in the actual market is different from each other.

2. *Tick-by-Tick Model*

There is a growing consensus that the volume traded and the price of a stock is correlated. This behavioral finance model attempts to explain the correlation between volume and price observed in high-frequency trading data at the tick-by-tick level. In this model, the investors' preferences are modeled by a random utility model which incorporates several important behavioral biases such as *status quo* bias, the disposition effect and loss aversion.

3. *Principal-agent Model*

Standard research into corporate finance is based on the assumption that agents are self-interested, rational utility-maximisers. For instance, the principal-agent problem that exists between investors and managers is based on selfish managerial rationality. Richard Fairchild (2004) examined the effect of behavioral factors, and specifically managerial irrationality, in capital budgeting. He developed a principal-agent model of capital budgeting which provides the basis for an experiment to test for three behavioral factors; reciprocal trust between an investor and a manager, framing behavior resulting in irrational commitment to a project that should be abandoned, and framing behavior combined with managerial overconfidence resulting in excessive effort levels.

4. *Black-Litterman Model*

Research has been performed within behavioral finance with respect to portfolio modeling. Shefrin and Statman (1997) and Massa and Simonov (2003) presented portfolio theories relating to behavior of private investors. According to the views of Charlotta Mankert (2006), the Black-Litterman model is a development of the Markowitz model. This model begins from the equilibrium portfolio approximated by the weights of the benchmark portfolio against which the fund manager is evaluated. Further, the investor inputs 'views', to which level of confidence is assigned by him/her. The resulting portfolio is then a combination of the benchmark portfolio and the view portfolio input by the investor. The weighting depends on the levels of confidence assigned to each view and the weight-on-views.

5. *Behavioral Asset Pricing Model (BAPM)*

The asset pricing model of standard finance is moving away from the capital asset pricing model in which beta is the only characteristic that determines expected stock returns towards a model that is similar to BAPM. One difference between the three-factor model of standard finance and the BAPM is in the interpretation of characteristics.

Microfinance Model

Microfinance is the provision of financial services like loans, savings and insurance to poor people, primarily in developing countries. It is a broad category of services, which includes microcredit. The microfinance products are tailored to be demographic, financial relationships and needs of the poor. In other words, microfinance means building financial systems that serve the poor.

The delivery mechanism of microcredit to the poor has created the idea of organizing Self-Help Groups. These SHGs collect voluntary savings on a regular basis and use the pooled resources to finance their members. Moreover, microfinance in India has witnessed a recent impetus with a growing number of commercially oriented microfinance institutions (MFIs) emerging and banks increasing their exposure to this sector considerably.

Cornford (2001) attempts to explain that, it is necessary to understand the distinctions between the more famous models of microfinance and more importantly, the context in which each evolved. They question that, how far the models can be accessed to financial services for the poor in the Pacific region. He throws open a discussion to the readers to consider the types of financial services and methods appropriate in the Pacific context. Dasgupta (2005) studied alternative models for microfinance in India. He disclosed that, one of the reasons for the lackluster performance of both public and private sector banks in extending credit to weaker sections is their high level of non performing assets. He found that growth in SHG credit has been uneven throughout the states of India. Besides discussing the model of SHG in extending credit to weaker sections, he also disclosed other different models that exist for extending microcredit to the poor and weaker sections. Ananth (2006) explained that, microfinance in India has witnessed a growing number of microfinance institutions and banks increasing their exposure to this sector considerably. The key focus of this paper is that of access of capital required for building a scaled microfinance industry. The paper observes that, the prevailing microfinance models tend to use risk capital inefficiently. Moreover, the performance of few MFIs identified to be at the low levels of average. This paper analyses the models of microfinance in India and intend to suggest a new approach developed by ICICI Bank. The Partnership model pioneered by ICICI Bank has been attempted in this paper to address some of the key gaps.

The below mentioned are some of the microfinance models that are in existence in Indian sub-continent, and as well as in other countries.

1. The SHG-Bank Linkage Model

This is a leading model in the Indian microfinance context that accounts for nearly 20 million clients. Under this model, the Self-Help Promoting Institution (SHPI), usually a Non-Government Organization promotes groups of 15 to 20 people which, after a certain incubation period, are attached to banks. The process of bank linkage involves the banks lending to groups after incubation period. This linkage may be single or multi-period. Once the groups have been linked to the bank, the SHPI may supervise the loan portfolio out of an implicit understanding with the bank as in the common case. However, the SHPI does not receive any specific incentive for playing its role and moreover, pricing to the clients under this model is not based on full costing.

2. Microfinance Institution Model (MFI Model)

According to this model given by NABARD in its report of 2006, the MFI borrows from commercial sources and lends to clients. This is a recent shift that has been facilitated in part by the participation of commercial banks in the microfinance sector and in part by the lack of resource options for growing MFIs. Most of MFIs in India started operations with grants and commercial loans and gradually made transition to commercial funding.

3. Bank Partnership Model

According to Bindu Ananth (2006), a report prepared by the ICICI bank after thorough analysis and also evidencing a consistent viable demand from the clients, the traditional method of organization-based financing model has constrained the exposure of MFIs. Moreover, the SHG-Bank Linkage model was not considered scalable way for ICICI Bank due to its limited number of rural branches. In light of the analysis done by the ICICI bank, it has developed a unique partnership model to deliver small loans to the poor. The bank's main objective was to reach thousands of poor people with tiny loans. In this model, the bank selects MFIs as partners who then act as managing agents for it. These partners are selected carefully with substantial outreach and high quality microfinance portfolios. These MFIs work through Self-Help Groups.

E-finance Model

E-finance is about web-enabled finance function, which includes all areas of the financial services industry. Technology enablers play key roles in making the transition to e-finance. E-finance allows banks, non-banks financial institutions and capital markets to reach far more borrowers, including small and medium-sized enterprises (SMEs). E-finance encompasses all financial products and services which are available to the consumer through the internet. In India, a few banks and financial institutions have realized the immense power of the internet and have taken bold initiatives to promote innovative products and services on the internet platform.

Christiansen (2001) explains about the economics and institutional factors of electronic finance. His intention is to shed additional light on recent trends in electronic financial services, with a special view to analyzing e-finance as an extension of financial operators' continuous efforts at various levels. Moreover, the study relates to the potential future use of e-finance as a tool for increasing cross-border competition between financial institutions. Lingfen *et al* (2010) examined recent trends in e-finance and have shown the growth of mobile technology. They explain that, the development of systems on mobile devices can require a lot more resources in the form of development time. Their objective was to compare the implementation process of developing on each mobile device. Finally, they recommended three mainstream mobile device platforms to examine their potential suitability for e-finance projects.

The below mentioned are some of the E-finance models in existence.

1. *Business-to-Business Model (B2B)*

This model includes services in corporate financing, investing, institutions and international finance issues such as foreign exchange, derivatives and new issues, and back-end processing.

2. *Business-to-Consumer Model (B2C)*

This model includes services such as online trading, basic online banking, electronic bill payment, mortgages and insurance.

3. *Consumer-to-Consumer Model (C2C) This model includes payment for online transactions and electronic money transfers (EMT).*

4. *Technology Services Model*

This model supports the e-finance platform integrating the Information Technology architecture of the firm with the internet platform as well as older legacy systems.

2. EXPLANATION OF DIFFERENT HYPOTHESES

The Structure of this Book

The validity of each of the models explained above on finance depends ultimately upon the supporting empirical evidence. In reviewing the models in finance, the chapters in this book draw on both conceptual and quantitative approaches to shed light on the contribution of these models to various aspects of finance.

Primarily using Indian evidence, the first quarter of the book (Chapters 2-7) examines the contribution of corporate financial aspects of cost of capital and the impact of liberalization on it, perspectives of mergers and acquisitions and their performance, a relative-value investment strategy of pairs-trading, identifying the inconvenient transactions of the auditors in vouching, and observing investors' perceptions on different financial instruments. The second quarter of the book (Chapters 8-11) looks at microfinance in various aspects. The third quarter of the book (Chapters 12-15) observes into the aspects of behavioral finance and e-finance including banks and financial sector crisis.

Chapters 2 and 3 examine two different aspects of corporate finance. In Chapter 2, Sukhwinder Kaur and Fulbag Singh address the liberalization policies of the Government of India which have been structured to revitalize the Indian industry by absorbing it with a greater degree of competition. By examining the reports of one of the leading companies ACC Limited in cement industry over a period of 31 years, i.e. 1979-80 to 2009-10, the importance of cost of capital has been explained. This chapter identifies the objectives of the leading company with respect to the liberalization policies and its impact on the cost of capital. The study in this chapter is two-fold, i.e. examining the impact on the cost of capital during pre-liberalization and post-liberalization periods. The chapter concludes a more positive signal by indicating a decline in the overall cost of capital during post-liberalization period as compared to pre-liberalization period.

In Chapter 3, Leepsa highlights the perspectives of mergers and acquisitions and also attempts to document the role played by these mergers and acquisitions in the growth and development of companies. By investigating the current trends of M&A over a period of 12 years, an attempt has been made to base the study on the chemical industry. The mission of this chapter marches towards the financial performance of selected chemical companies basing upon parameters of liquidity, solvency and profitability in the post-merger period. This chapter finally drops the curtain by disclosing that, mergers have no impact on the financial performance of the chemical companies.

Chapters 4 and 5 address a relative-value investment strategy and perceptions of auditors. First, Raghu and Hari Babu , in Chapter 4, review an unpublicized market neutral strategy but a successful approach among institutional fund managers and hedge fund experts. They highlight an investment strategy that quests to identify two companies with similar characteristics whose equity securities are currently trading at a price relationship. They intend to identify the pairs of stocks exhibiting profits and conserving estimates of transactions cost with the help of previously documented literature. They provide evidence that, the pairs trading strategy has been viewed as a low profitability due to increased activity of hedge funds and also documented that this strategy is not trouble-free. Second, Prakash and Renu, in Chapter 5, provides an overview of accounting transactions that take place in an entity and explained the examination of those accounts by the auditors as an important task. The duty of the auditors has been explained where they have to verify the assets and liabilities with the help of vouching. Their identification dwells the most inconvenient transactions of the auditors in relation to vouching, provide concrete suggestions, and locate prime objective of verifying assets and liabilities. Their conclusion confronts that, some transactions in debit side of the cash book, credit side of the cash book and impersonal ledger are most ponderous to be evaluated with the help of documentary evidences and further they documented that the auditors are in a dilemma in examining rough cash book.

Chapters 6 and 7 focus on increased investment which is riskier and mitigation of financial risk. In Chapter 6, Surya Prakasha and Hari Babu examined the riskier investments taking into account some safety measures to increase the level of security of the investments. They observed that, financial instruments are more profitable than saving in a bank because of the multiplication of assets. They also studied several factors that make the investment riskier. Their intention is to publicize the investors' perception on financial instruments that leads to increase in investment. To make aware of this, they incorporated a case study of Warren Buffet in this chapter. Their study comes to an end by disclosing certain facts that, investors' main perception is on those instruments that include the benefit of capital appreciation, tax benefits and risk-free return. Minaketan and Sasikantha consider corporate governance to mitigate financial risks in Chapter 7. They lifted the curtain by observing that, improved corporate earnings are being affected due to the improper management of financial risk. Their study landed over the banking industry because it is an organized and regulated one and also several reforms have been initiated in this sector. They intend to show a bird's eye view about the concept of corporate governance and its ethical issues and opportunities to mitigate financial risk in the banking sector. Also they intend to analyze the impact of financial risks on the economic environment and sustainability of India. Their study concluded with an argument that, protection of depositors in developing economies is undermined due to lack of well-trained supervisors, inadequate disclosure requirements, and the cost of raising bank capital and also they documented that corporate governance is not playing as a risk management tool.

Chapters 8 to 11 address aspects of microfinance in various dimensions. Issues relating to microfinance risks and SKS microfinance are addressed in Chapters 8 and 9. Shalini explains about the microfinance industry during the last decade in terms of its breadth, depth and scope in Chapter 8. She observes about the continuity of rapid growth, given the massive un-served and underserved market. Further, she also observed the changed risk profile of MFIs by the growth of the industry. The intention of the author is to explore the importance and value of risk management to MFIs and to design a framework for managing these risks systematically. The author ended up her views by suggesting a concrete approach called CAMEL introduced by ACCION a global NGO to make the MFI financially sound and to mitigate the financial risk of MFIs. In Chapter 9, Manoj attempts to explain about the working and performance of SKS Microfinance which is a microfinance financial institution. He took an opportunity to re-infuse a quotation of 2004 by saying 'banks are for people with money, not for people without'. The establishment and working of SKS Microfinance are viewed in a very legible manner. Moreover, the financial performance of the said financial institution, its wide-spread branches, HR strategies was also considered. Further, the borrowings and disbursement of finance by this institution has been observed. The current study has also observed the obstacles faced by the said financial institution in its growth journey. The chapter comes to an end by disclosing certain facts that, SKS Microfinance is a responsible leader following ethical practices and processes in dealing with borrowers and on the other hand offered suggestions to overcome the hurdles of growth.

The way the microfinance engenders the socio-economic, cultural change and empowers women has been addressed conceptually in Chapters 10 and 11. Nandita attempts to disclose the facts of empowering of women through microfinance in Chapter 10. She discussed about the role of women in the Indian society, the way government and non-government organizations contributed in their development. She observed that women are significant contributors to the growing economy. She disclosed the barriers faced by women to access education, health, employment, etc. She also mentioned that, women make up the majority of low paid, unorganized informal sector of most economies. The intention of this chapter is to discuss the role of microfinance in women empowerment and further to focus on the changes brought by microfinance in women's life. She highlighted the role of SHG-Bank linkage program for the empowerment of women. The paper concludes by saying that, the lives of women were transformed from rural to full-time entrepreneurs and with a self-esteem life with the support of SHGs. Moreover, it has also been mentioned that, women are in a position to contribute their intelligence for the development of the nation. In Chapter 11, the issues of rural women belonging to economically and socially weaker sections of the society have been highlighted by Sreevidya. She attempts to show the conditions that do not permit women to meet minimum consumption needs, and also the way these women depend on rural money lenders for their consumption needs has been discussed. She discloses that, the formation of SHGs has shown promising results and also they have been prove as poverty reduction method bringing socio-economic and cultural changes among marginalized communities. She intends to explore the role played by the financial institutions in providing loans to SHGs and also to identify the socio-cultural changes due to the involvement of women in self-help groups. The study found that, the rise of SHGs and microfinance made the women belonging to weaker sections to resort to habitual savings and to have easy access to credit. At the end it was concluded that, various programs and provisions act as concomitant accelerating factors and processes bring mobility and change among weaker sections of the society and it was also mentioned that, changes may take place in the socio-cultural system due to technological innovations.

In the final of the four chapters dealing with psychological behavior of investors and innovative finance including banking, Chapter 12, Manish examines the investment choice of university teachers of DAVV. He attempts to explain that, investment choice differs from person to person, as every individual is affected by his own socio-economic characteristics which defines his needs and objectives and ultimately guides his investment choice. Moreover, the level of investment awareness and previous investment experiences stand as an important factor guiding choice of investment. His exploration includes investment choice of teachers and association between their individualistic and profession related demographic variables. He established a basic proposition that, university teachers, like other individuals, are affected by general individual demography and there is no association of professional-related demography with their investment choice. The findings of his research discloses that, the gender, age, qualification, existing wealth and investment experience found to be significantly associated with investment choice whereas, the profession-related demographic variables are not significantly associated with investment choice. The chapter concludes by saying that, investors do not behave rationally and their choice of investment is decided by demographic factors. In Chapter 13, Atul and Monica addresses investor behavior in portfolio management. They attempted to discover the fact that, when it comes to investing, even rational people sometimes make foolish and irrational decisions. They intend to explain the evolution of behavioral finance, and the way it considers the influence of personal and social psychology on financial decisions and the behavior of financial markets. They also disclosed some key aspects of behavior finance and investors' biases. Their exploration includes, finding out various investors' biases that influence decision-making process and also how various factors related to them affect stock markets. They also intend to describe various practical applications of behavioral finance. Their study concluded by conveying that, there is no concrete set of theory or a model of investor behavior and that theory does not help people beat the market, but their psychology causes market prices and fundamental values to diverge.

The last two chapters address issues of banking and finance sector and banking transformation through technology. Roshni and Sasikantha, in Chapter 14, examine banking and finance sector in the era of economic meltdown and strategic dimensions and directions during that period. They attempt to address the economic slowdown and its impact on various sectors. They say that, the Central Government and the RBI are trying their best to infuse liquidity by giving certain relaxations to the industries to give stimulus to the economy. Their intention is to take a closer look at the counter strategies taken by banks in the times of crisis and economic meltdown. Moreover, they also focus on the win-win situation of the banks during the crisis. They disclosed various strategies adopted by the banks during the time of crisis and economic meltdown. They finally disclosed that, the financial downturn has made successful banks returned to their bins, compelled governments to recapitalize and raised questions about risk management.

Titus and Mathew, in Chapter 15, examine the transformation of banking through technology driven mobility. They attempt to address that, banks are making a continuous effort to provide customer-centric services at reduced costs and ensure operational efficiency to the greatest extent. Moreover, the advent of internet has initiated a digital revolution in the world-wide banking sector. A new banking platform offering entirely new types of banking services have emerged innovating on various on e-business models carving a way for mobile banking. Their intention is to explore mobile banking and its practice with the help of futuristic model. Their research work also navigates the service value propositions that are being built for consumers through the use of mobile banking. They proposed a model called Banking Information Systems Model, which enhances the value of two key stakeholders, namely the banking institution and the service user (customer). They concluded the paper by saying that, people will enjoy the banking services like never before in the future and the mobile device will slowly morph into a ubiquitous payment device. Finally, financial institutions will be better positioned by implementing an enterprise-wide mobile financial services platform.

References

Affan, S., (2008). Financial Modeling and Corporate Valuations, http://www.icap.org.pk/userfiles/file/presentation/financial_modelling_corporate.pdf accessed on 19/08/2012.

Ananth, B., (2006). Financing Microfinance: The ICICI Bank Partnership Model, Towards a Sustainable Microfinance Outreach in India (Experiences and Perspectives), 227-239.

Cornell, B., and Shapiro, A.C. (1987). Corporate Stakeholders and Corporate Finance, *Financial Management*, Vol. 16(1), 5-14.

Cornford, R., (2001). 'Microcredit', 'Microfinance' or 'access to financial services' What do Pacific people need?, The Foundation for Development Cooperation.

Chriastiansen, H., (2001). Electronic Finance: Economics and Institutional Factors, http://paris-europlace.net/files/news059121.pdf accessed on 12/08/2012.

Dasgupta, R., (2005). Microfinance in India: Empirical Evidence, Alternative Models and Policy Imperatives, *Economic and Political Weekly*, Vol. 40(12), 1229-37.

Dermiguc, A., and Levine, R. (1996). Stock Market, Corporate Finance, and Economic Growth: An Overview, *The World Bank Economic Review*, Vol. 10(2), 223-39.

Fairchild, R., (2004). Behavioral Finance in a Principal-agent model of Capital Budgeting, Working Paper Series, School of Management, University of Bath.

Graham, J.R., and Harvey, C.R. (2001). The Theory and Practice of Corporate Finance: Evidence from the field, *Journal of Financial Economics*, Vol. 60, 187-243.

Heaton, J.B., (2002). Managerial Optimism and Corporate Finance, *Financial Management*, Vol. 31(2), 33-45.

Iyengar, G., and Chun, A. (2010). A Behavioral Finance-based tick-by-tick model for price and volume, *The Journal of Computational Finance*, Vol. 14(1), 57-80.

Lingfen, C., Woods, D., Curran, K., and Doherty, J. (2010). Mobile Development Environments for Electronic Finance, *International Journal of Electronic Finance*, Vol. 4(2), 99-119.

Mankert, C., (2006). The Black-Litterman Model—mathematical and behavioral finance approaches towards its use in practice, Thesis, Royal Institute of Technology, Sweden.

Ramesh, T., and Venkateshwarlu, M. (2011). A New Quantitative Behavioral Model for Financial Prediction, 3rd International Conference on Information and Financial Engineering, Singapore.

Ritter, J.R., (2003). Behavioral Finance, *Pacific-Basin Finance Journal*, Vol. 11 (4), 429-37.

Shefrin, H., (2001). Behavioral Corporate Finance, *Journal of Applied Corporate Finance*, Vol. 14(3).

Statman, M., (1999), Behavioral Finance: Past Battles and Future Engagements, *Financial Analysts Journal*, Vol. 55(6), 18-27.

2

Impact of Liberalization on Cost of Capital—A Case Study of the Associated Cement Companies Limited

DR. SUKHWINDER KAUR AND DR. FULBAG SINGH

INTRODUCTION

Liberalization policies of the Government of India have been structured to revitalize the Indian industry by infusing it with a greater degree of competition. As opposed to earlier policies which directed investment in industry to what were understood to be 'nationally desirous' in a protected environment. Liberalization allows a manufacturer greater liberty in selecting investment levels and output patterns according to the dictates of the market. Liberalization policies in India have a modest beginning in the late 1960s to remedy the foreign exchange and fiscal problems faced by the economy. The first was the prolonged stagnation in the industrial sector. The second was increasing inefficiency and low rates of return of the public sector as a whole into which the Government has committed vast resources resulting in an internal resource crunch. The third was the recurring balance of payments crisis. A conscious policy of liberalization was advanced by policy-makers as an effective measure to counter these problems. Liberalization by systematically deregulating industry and cutting down restrictions on trade (especially imports) aimed at infusing greater competition into the industrial sector and thereby led to increase in growth and efficiency.

The Indian financial system has undergone transformation over the last four decades and now comprises of an impressive network of financial institutions, financial markets and a wide range of financial instruments. Developing countries have progressively adopted market-friendly reforms during 1980s and 1990s. One of the most important objectives of these reforms was to make economies more resilient and less vulnerable to external shocks. More than 20 years have passed, since the Indian Government has started the process of liberalization and now almost all sectors are reaping the harvest of economic and financial sector reforms. Financial sector liberalization can be viewed as a set of operational reforms and policy measures designed to deregulate and transform the financial system and its structure with a view to achieve a liberalized market-oriented system with an appropriate regulatory framework. The liberalization process undertaken in the country has resulted in a wide range of changes and adoption of market policies that spanned the whole economy. Changes have taken place in almost all important sectors of the economy including capital markets, banking sector and industrial sector. The primary motive behind liberalization was to impart greater depth, liquidity and stability of financial Institutions and markets. The Government of India also launched reform programmes for capital market in 1991. The reforms in capital market enabled firms to raise funds cheaply and contributed to the diversification of corporate finance. In 1992, CCI was abolished and thereafter, Securities and Exchange Board of India (SEBI) became a regulatory body with an explicit mandate of protecting investors and developing the capital market. The lending and borrowing behavior of Indian companies as well as financing patterns have undergone change as a result of economic and financial liberalization in 1991. The pattern of capital structure, i.e. choice of different proportions of the financing mix affects the efficiency of a business enterprise. Mainly capital structure of a company has to be viewed with respect to risk, return and cost being attached to each source of financing mix. Cost of capital for a firm is the average rate of return that the investors in a firm would expect for supplying funds to firm or in other words, it is the cost of obtaining funds. It is the cut-off rate for allocation of capital to the investment of projects that will leave unchanged the market price of a stock **(Van Horne, 2002)**. The excessive use of debt may endanger the survival of firm while its conservative use may deprive the equity shareholders from magnifying their return by using debt as cheaper source of finance. Thus, the importance of an appropriate and sound capital structure with low cost of capital is obvious from the perspective of corporate enterprises, its owners and other stakeholders. In the present study an attempt has been made to study the cost of capital of one of the leading companies in cement industry, i.e. Associated Cement Companies (ACC) Limited over the study period of 31 years. The entire study period has been segregated into two parts: Pre-liberalization Period (1979-80 to 1989-90) and Post-liberalization Period (1990-91 to 2009-10).

OBJECTIVES OF THE STUDY

The main objective of this case study is to have insight into the cost of capital of ACC Limited. The specific objectives of the study are as follows:

- To analyze trends in leverage ratios (L_1, L_2, L_3 and L_4) over the study period of 31 years, i.e. 1979-80 to 2009-10.
- To study trends in cost of debt (K_{dat}), cost of preference share capital (K_p), cost of equity capital (K_{e1} and K_{e2}) and overall cost of capital (K_{o1} and K_{o2}) over the study period of 31 years, i.e. 1979-80 to 2009-10.
- To analyze the effect of liberalization upon cost of capital.

OVERVIEW OF ASSOCIATED CEMENT COMPANIES LIMITED

Associated Cement Companies Limited (ACC) is one of the leading companies in the cement industry. It was incorporated in 1936 at Bombay. The company was incorporated with the objective of manufacture of cement, refractories, cement plant and other heavy machinery including structural and mild fabrications. When this company was incorporated on August 1, 1936 from the merger of 10 cement companies, its formation was hailed as "the beginning of a new era in the Indian Cement Industry" and it instantly became one of the largest Indian companies of the time. ACC Ltd. has played a vital role in the development of a vibrant India. Now the organization has entered its seventy-fifth year. As the platinum jubilee year unfolds, the company is on the threshold of a new phase of growth, armed with ultramodern production facilities, including the world's largest cement kiln at Wadi. Among the first companies in India to include commitment to environment protection as a corporate objective, ACC Ltd. vigorously pursues its goal of sustainable development through exacting standards in environmental conservation, emission controls, maximizing energy efficiency, the promotion of renewable energy, the pursuit of alternative fuels and raw materials, waste management, clean mining techniques and of course safety. ACC Ltd. has played a vital role in the development of a vibrant India. The company has put in over seven decades of dedicated efforts in helping build infrastructure, ushering in modern distribution and construction practices. At present ACC has become a name synonymous with trust and confidence.

DATA BASE AND METHODOLOGY

The financial data for the purpose of the present study have been collected from The Bombay Stock Exchange Official Directory, Prowess database maintained by Centre for Monitoring Indian Economy (CMIE) and annual reports of selected companies. The ratio of funded debt (long-term debt) to equity (D_1/E_1), funded debt plus preference capital to equity ($(D_1+P)/E_2$), interest bearing debt to equity (D_2/E_1) and total debt (long-term loans plus short-term loans including current liabilities) to equity (D_3/E_1) respectively are taken as four measures of leverage for the present study. Equity here represents paid up share capital plus reserves and surpluses reduced by fictitious assets. E_1 above represent equity including preference capital and E_2 represent equity excluding preference capital. The overall cost of capital in terms of (K_{o1} and K_{o2}) of this company is computed by taking into account respective cost of debt after tax (K_{dat}), cost of preference share capital (K_p) and cost of equity capital (K_{e1} and K_{e2}) (including cost of common stock plus cost of retained earnings) multiplied by their respective weights in the financing mix of company. The entire period of study has been segregated into two parts, i.e. pre-liberalization period (1979-80 to 1989-90) and post-liberalization period (1990-91 to 2009-10). The mathematical and statistical techniques such as ratio analysis, percentages, compound growth rate and multiple regression analysis have been used for the purpose of analysis of collected data. The data have been objectively analyzed and conclusions are drawn on the basis of parametric tests at 1 percent, 5 percent and 10 percent levels of significance respectively. All calculations have been done by using SPSS version 16 on the computer. The following formulas have been used to compute the cost of each specific source of finance and overall cost of capital (K_{o1} and K_{o2})

The cost of debt after tax (K_{dat}) is calculated by following formula:

$$K_{dat} = K_{dbt}\ (1\text{-}t)$$

where,

$$K_{dbt} = \frac{\text{Annual Interest Payable}}{\text{Average Debt}}$$,, i.e. Cost of debt before tax

$$\text{Avg. Debt} = \frac{\text{Intt. Bearing Debt at the end of curr. year} + \text{Intt. Bearing Debt at the end of prev. year}}{2}$$

Intt. Bearing Debt=Long-Term Intt. Bearing Debt + Short Term Intt. Bearing Debt

$$t = \text{Effective Tax Rate} = \frac{\text{Tax Provision}}{\text{Pre-Tax Profit}}$$

The cost of preference share capital (K_p) is calculated on the basis of preference dividend payable to preference shareholders. Since the data regarding floatation cost, discount or premium concerning issue and redemption is not available, the cost of preference share capital (K_p) has been worked out by using the following formula:

$$K_p = \frac{PD}{PC}$$

where, K_p represents the cost of preference share capital, PD refers to preference dividend and PC stands for paid up preference share capital.

Earnings model taking into account annual anticipated growth in earnings per share and compound growth in earnings per share on a five year basis has been taken as the base for computation of cost of equity capital (K_{e1} and K_{e2}) for the present study.

$$K_{e1} = \frac{EPS_1}{P_o} + g$$

EPS_1 = EPS_o (1+g).
EPS_1 = Expected earnings per share at the end of the year.
EPS_o = Earnings per share for the previous year.
P_o = Average market price of share at the end of previous year.
g = Annual growth rate in earnings per share.

$$K_{e2} = K_{e1} = \frac{EPS_1}{P_o} + g$$

EPS_1 = EPS_o (1+g).
EPS_1 = Expected earnings per share at the end of the year.

EPS_o = Earnings per share for the previous year.
P_o = Average market price of share at the end of previous year.
g = Compound Growth rate in earnings per share computed on a five year basis.

In order to estimate growth rates statistically taking five-year basis, logarithms of both sides of equations set for earnings per share are taken. This equation is linear in logarithms and has a slope equal to log (1+g). Using the least squares regression technique, we can estimate log (1+g).

$$\log(1+g) = \frac{\sum_{t=1}^{n} y_t \log EPS_t}{\sum_{t=1}^{n} y_t^2}$$

The overall cost of capital in terms of (K_{o1} and K_{o2}) is computed by taking into account respective cost of debt (K_{dat}), cost of preference share capital (K_p) and cost of equity capital (K_{e1} and K_{e2}) multiplied by their respective weights in the financing mix of the company.

$$K_{o1} = K_{dat} W_d + K_p W_p + K_{e1} W_e$$
$$K_{o2} = K_{dat} W_d + K_p W_p + K_{e2} W_e$$

Where, K_{o1}, K_{o2}, K_{e1} and K_{e2} represent the overall cost of capital and cost of equity capital computed on the basis of earnings model taking into account annual anticipated growth in earnings per share and compound growth in earnings per share respectively, whereas K_{dat}, and K_p represent respective the cost of debt after tax and cost of preference share capital. W_d, W_p and W_e represent respective weights of each source in the financing mix of the company.

MEASURES FOR THE VARIABLES

Size (S_1 and S_2), leverage (L_1, L_2, L_3, L_4), non-debt tax shields, reserves and retained earnings to total assets, liquidity, growth (G_1, G_2 and G_3), profitability (P_1 and P_2), collaterals and age respectively are taken as independent variables, whereas the overall cost of capital in terms of (K_{o1}) and (K_{o2}) represent dependent variables for the present study. The natural logarithm of net sales and total assets is taken as two measures of size (S_1 and S_2) in the present study. L_1, L_2, L_3 and L_4

respectively are taken as four measures of leverage in the present study. Liquidity is measured by the ratio of current assets to current liabilities. Annual percentage increase in net sales, total assets and earnings before interest and taxes (EBIT) have been taken as three measure of growth (G_1, G_2 and G_3) in the present study. Two measures of profitability (P_1 and P_2) are used in the present study. Profitability is measured in terms of earnings before interest and taxes to net sales and earnings before interest and taxes to total assets. The ratio of net fixed assets to total assets is used to measure collaterals in the present study. Age is measured in terms of the number of years since incorporation.

ANALYSIS

Table 1 represents trends in D_1/E_1, $(D_1+P)/E_2$, D_2/E_1 and D_3/E_1 ratios for pre-liberalization and post-liberalization periods separately and then for entire period of study covering 31 years. The D/E ratio of 2:1 is considered to be standard norm for all companies incorporated in India. The D_1/E_1, $(D_1+P)/E_2$, D_2/E_1 and D_3/E_1 ratios of ACC Ltd. range between 0.39 in 1979-80 to 1.67 in 1984-85, from 0.39 in 1979-80 to 1.67 in 1984-85, from 1.19 in 1979-80 to 2.29 in 1988-89 and from 2.77 in 1985-86 to 3.58 in 1989-90 respectively during pre-liberalization period. These ratios have exhibited an increasing trend in 10 years, 10 years, 10 years and 7 years respectively out of 11 years as compared with the first year of the study during this period. These ratios range between 0.06 in 2006-07 to 1.36 in 2002-03, from 0.06 in 2006-07 to 1.36 in 2002-03, from 0.07 in 2006-07 to 1.68 in 2001-02 and from 0.60 in 2008-09 to 2.83 in 1993-94 respectively during post-liberalization period. These ratios have exhibited an increasing trend in 10 years, 10 years and 11 years respectively out of 20 years during this period. The D_3/E_1 ratio has exhibited a declining trend in 12 out of 20 years during this period. These respective ratios range between 0.06 in 2006-07 to 1.67 in 1984-85, from 0.07 in 2006-07 to 2.29 in 1988-89, and from 0.60 in 2008-09 to 3.58 in 1989-90 respectively over the study period. These ratios have exhibited an increasing trend in 26 years, 26 years and 19 years respectively out of 31 years over the study period. The D_3/E_1 ratio has exhibited declining trend in 22 out of 31 years over the study period. From the Table 1 it has been observed that ACC Ltd. prefers to have low D/E ratio thus creating additional debt capacity and enabling the company to raise further funds by way of debt or equity in case of adverse capital market conditions. The company also has advantage of raising funds by way of equity at high premium due to less financial risk.

TABLE I

Analysis of Various Debt to Equity Ratios of ACC Ltd. during 1979-80 to 2009-10

Year	D_l/E_l	$(D_l+P_l)/E$	D_l/E_2	D_l/E_2
Pre-Liberalization Period				
1979-80	**0.39**	**0.39**	**1.19**	2.82
1980-81	1.13	1.13	1.92	3.74
1981-82	**1.15**	**1.15**	**1.71**	3.28
1982-83	0.97	0.97	1.43	2.72
1983-84	1.36	1.36	1.77	3.00
1984-85	**1.67**	**1.67**	1.69	2.90
1985-86	1.14	1.14	1.55	**2.77**
1986-87	1.08	1.08	1.59	2.89
1987-88	1.03	1.03	1.58	2.80
1988-89	1.81	1.81	**2.29**	3.92
1989-90	1.53	1.53	1.99	**3.58**
Post-Liberalization Period				
1990-91	0.84	0.84	1.06	2.06
1991-92	0.81	0.81	1.07	2.14
1992-93	1.13	1.13	1.50	2.63
1993-94	1.19	1.19	1.71	**2.83**
1994-95	0.78	0.78	1.26	2.09
1995-96	0.75	0.75	0.68	1.31
1996-97	0.95	0.95	0.94	1.44
1997-98	0.92	0.92	1.55	2.03
1998-99	0.97	0.97	1.46	1.96
1999-00	1.00	1.00	1.38	1.98
2000-01	0.95	0.95	1.59	2.13
2001-02	1.23	1.23	**1.68**	2.33
2002-03	**1.36**	**1.36**	1.46	2.16
2003-04	1.09	1.09	1.09	1.71
2004-05	0.66	0.66	0.96	1.58
2005-06	0.49	0.49	0.50	1.13
2006-07	**0.06**	**0.06**	**0.07**	0.61
2007-08	0.09	0.09	0.10	0.65
2008-09	0.09	0.09	0.09	**0.60**
2009-10	0.08	0.08	0.08	0.66

Source: Compiled and Analyzed from the Basic Data Obtained from Bombay Stock Exchange Official Directory, Prowess Database (CMIE) and Annual Reports of Companies.

Table 2 presents trends in cost of each specific source of finance and overall cost of capital (K_{o1} and K_{o2}) for pre-liberalization period, post-liberalization period and over the entire period of study covering 31 years. The trends in cost of capital have been studied with the help of compound growth rates. The compound growth rates have been computed for cost of each specific source of finance and the overall cost of capital (K_{o1} and K_{o2}) for pre-liberalization period, post-liberalization period and over the study period of 31 years. The compound growth rate of cost of debt (K_{dat}) of ACC Ltd. has been observed 6.28 percent during pre-liberalization period. It turns negative to the extent of 5.06 percent during the post-liberalization period. Such type of trend indicates decline in cost of debt (K_{dat}) during post-liberalization period as compared to pre-liberalization period. The compound growth rate of cost of debt (K_{dat}) has been observed negative to the extent of 1.77 percent over the study period. It is a healthy sign as it indicates decline in cost of debt (K_{dat}) during the study period. This company does not have preference share capital (K_p) over the study period. The compound growth rate of cost of equity capital (K_{e1}) has been observed as 22.34 percent during pre-liberalization period. It has been observed negative to the extent of 3.66 percent during post-liberalization period. The compound growth rate of cost of equity capital (K_{e1}) has been observed 2.73 percent over the study period of 31 years. It is not a healthy sign as it indicates an increase in cost of equity capital (K_{e1}) during the study period. The compound growth rate of cost of equity capital (K_{e2}) has been observed negative to the extent of 8.57 percent, 0.38 percent and 2.82 percent respectively during pre-liberalization period, post-liberalization period and over the entire study period respectively. This type of trend indicates decline in cost of equity capital (K_{e2}) during the study period. The compound growth rate of overall cost of capital (K_{o1}) has reduced from 11.65 percent in pre-liberalization period to -3.7 percent during post-liberalization period. Such type of trend indicates decline in overall cost of capital (K_{o1}) during post-liberalization period as compared to pre-liberalization period. The overall cost of capital (K_{o1}) has exhibited an increase of 0.32 percent over the entire study period. The compound growth rate of overall cost of capital (K_{o2}) has been observed negative to the extent of 6.09 percent during pre-liberalization period. It has been observed 0.86 percent during post-liberalization period. This type of trend indicates an increase in overall cost of capital (K_{o2}) during post-liberalization period as compared to pre-liberalization period. The overall cost of capital (K_{o2}) has exhibited decline of -0.86 percent over the entire period of study covering 31 years.

TABLE 2

Trend Analysis of Cost of Capital of Associated Cement Co. Ltd. during 1979-80 to 2009-10

Year	K_{dat} (%)	K_p (%)	K_{e1} (%)	K_{e2}* (%)	K_{o1} (%)	K_{o2} (%)
Pre-liberalization Period						
1979-80	7.30	0.00	2.50		5.11	
1980-81	7.98	0.00	14.47		10.20	
1981-82	7.33	0.00	17.81		11.20	
1982-83	9.29	0.00	26.04		16.19	
1983-84	13.24	0.00	17.08		14.63	
1984-85	14.99	0.00	11.93	50.80	13.85	28.32
1985-86	14.07	0.00	11.77	62.64	13.17	33.13
1986-87	13.39	0.00	10.15	17.39	12.14	14.93
1987-88	13.68	0.00	27.08	0.30	18.87	8.50
1988-89	8.36	0.00	12.44	12.44	9.60	9.60
1989-90	14.27	0.00	22.97	29.67	17.18	19.42
Post-liberalization Period						
1990-91	11.83	0.00	12.15	26.03	11.98	18.71
1991-92	6.15	0.00	22.14	47.71	13.87	26.22
1992-93	8.82	0.00	35.13	35.13	19.33	19.33
1993-94	9.00	0.00	57.12	57.12	26.78	26.78
1994-95	10.84	0.00	29.83	51.73	19.24	28.93
1995-96	12.13	0.00	19.26	43.71	16.38	30.95
1996-97	10.72	0.00	36.61	59.18	24.05	35.67
1997-98	6.68	0.00	8.91	8.91	7.55	7.55
1998-99	9.87	0.00	48.98	39.08	25.74	21.73
1999-00	11.20	0.00	2.09	2.09	7.38	7.38
2000-01	9.18	0.00	2.23	2.23	6.49	6.49
2001-02	7.30	0.00	8.25	8.25	7.65	7.65
2002-03	7.84	0.00	2.60	2.60	5.71	5.71
2003-04	6.12	0.00	19.39	5.24	12.45	5.70
[illegible]	[illegible]	[illegible]	[illegible]	[illegible]	[illegible]	[illegible]
2005-06	4.88	0.00	44.08	4.66	30.96	4.74
2006-07	5.53	0.00	32.03	45.93	30.21	43.16
2007-08	5.99	0.00	13.88	63.02	13.18	57.94
2008-09	7.05	0.00	45.99	48.24	42.64	44.69
2009-10	4.19	0.00	5.76	24.13	5.64	22.63
Compound Growth Rate (Pre-lib)	6.28	Nil	22.34	-8.57	11.65	-6.09
Compound Growth Rate (Post-lib)	-5.06	Nil	-3.66	-0.38	-3.7	0.96
Compound Growth Rate (Overall)	-1.77	Nil	2.73	-2.82	0.32	-0.86

Note: * = g for K_{e2} has been Computed as Compound Annualized Growth rate in Earnings per Share on Five-Year Basis (1979-80 to 1983-84) and so on. Hence K_{e2} has been computed from 1984-85 onwards.

Source: Compiled and Analyzed from the Basic Data Obtained from Bombay Stock Exchange Official Directory, Prowess Database (CMIE) and Annual Reports of Companies.

From the Table 2 it has been observed that the cost of debt (K_{dat}) of ACC Ltd. ranges between 7.30 percent in the year 1979-80 to 14.99 percent in the year 1984-85 during the pre-liberalization period. There has been an increase in 10 out of 11 years as compared to first year of the study period. An increasing trend has been observed in cost of debt (K_{dat}) over the study period. The cost of debt (K_{dat}) ranges between 4.19 percent in the year 2009-10 to 12.13 percent in the year 1995-96 during post-liberalization period. There has been decline in 18 out of 20 years as compared to first year of the study period. The cost of debt (K_{dat}) ranges between 4.19 percent in the year 2009-10 to 14.99 percent in the year 1984-85 over the study period of 31 years. There has been an increase in 21 out of 31 years as compared to first year of the study period. An increasing trend has been observed in cost of debt (K_{dat}) over the study period. This company does not have preference share capital during the study period.

The cost of equity share capital (K_{e1}) ranges between 2.50 percent in the year 1979-80 to 27.08 percent in the year 1987-88 during pre-liberalization period. There has been an increase in 10 out of 11 years as compared to first year of the study period. The cost of equity share capital (K_{e1}) has exhibited an increasing trend during this period. The cost of equity share capital (K_{e1}) ranges between 2.09 percent in the year 1999-00 to 57.12 percent in the year 1993-94 during the post-liberalization period. There has been an increase in 12 out of 20 years as compared to first year of the study period. An increasing trend has been observed in cost of equity share capital (K_{e1}) during this period. The cost of equity share capital (K_{e1}) ranges between 2.09 percent in the year 1999-00 to 57.12 percent in the year 1993-94 over the study period of 31 years. There has been increase in 28 out of 31 years as compared to first year of the study period. An increasing trend has been observed in cost of equity share capital (K_{e1}) during this period.

The cost of equity share capital (K_{e2}) ranges between 2.30 percent in the year 1987-88 to 62.64 percent in the year 1985-86 during pre-liberalization period. There has been decline in 4 out of 6 years as compared to first year of the study period. The cost of equity share capital (K_{e2}) has exhibited declining trend during this period. The cost of equity share capital (K_{e2}) ranges between 2.09 percent in the year 1999-00 to 63.02 percent in the year 2007-08 during post-liberalization period. It exhibits an increase in 10 out of 20 years as compared to first year of the study period. An increasing trend has been observed in cost of equity share capital (K_{e2}) during this period. The cost of equity share capital (K_{e2}) ranges between 2.09 percent in the year 1999-00 to 57.12 percent in the year 1993-94 over the entire study period. There has been decline in 20 out of 26 years as compared to first year of the study period. A declining trend has been observed in cost of equity share capital (K_{e2}) during this period.

The overall cost of capital (K_{o1}) ranges between 5.11 percent in the year 1979-80 to 18.87 percent in the year 1987-88 during pre-liberalization period. There has been an increase in 10 out of 11 years as compared to first year of the study period. An increasing trend has been observed in the overall cost of capital (K_{o1}) during this period. The overall cost of capital (K_{o1}) ranges between 5.64 percent in the year 2009-10 to 42.64 percent in the year 2008-09 during post-liberalization period. The overall cost of capital (K_{o1}) has exhibited an increase in 12 out of 20 years as compared to first year of the study period. An increasing trend has been observed in the overall cost of capital (K_{o1}) during this period. The overall cost of capital (K_{o1}) ranges between 5.11 percent in the year 1979-80 to 42.64 percent in the year 2008-09 over the study period of 31 years. There has been an increase in 30 out of 31 years as compared to first year of the study period. An increasing trend has been observed in overall cost of capital (K_{o1}) during this period.

The overall cost of capital (K_{o2}) ranges between 8.50 percent in the year 1987-88 to 33.13 percent in the year 1985-86 during pre-liberalization period. There has been decline in 4 out of 6 years as compared to first year of the study period. A declining trend has been observed in the overall cost of capital (K_{o1}) during this period. The overall cost of capital (K_{o1}) ranges between 4.74 percent in the year 2005-06 to 57.94 percent in the year 2007-08 during post-liberalization period. The overall cost of capital (K_{o1}) has exhibited an increase in 11 out of 20 years as compared to first year of the study period. An increasing trend has been observed in overall cost of capital (K_{o1}) during this period. The overall cost of capital (K_{o1}) ranges between 4.74 percent in the year 2005-06 to 57.94 percent in the year 2007-08 over the study period of 26 years. There has been decline in 18 out of 26 years as compared to first year of the study period. A declining trend has been observed in the overall cost of capital (K_{o2}) during this period.

From the above analysis it is interesting to note that there has been wide variations in cost of debt (K_{dat}), cost of preference share capital (K_p), cost of equity capital (K_{e1} and K_{e2}) and the overall cost of capital (K_{o1} and K_{o2}) over a period of time but the basic trend has been decline in respective costs during post-liberalization period. The cost of debt (K_{dat}) and cost of preference share capital (K_p) have been observed to be less than cost of equity capital (K_{e1} and K_{e2}) in maximum number of years in the present study. The fundamental reason behind the cost of debt (K_{dat}) being less than cost of equity (K_e) is due to lower risk premium and tax advantage of debt has been accepted as per findings of the present study. The findings of this study support the traditional viewpoint of capital structure theories that with the judicious use of debt, the overall cost of capital (K_o) is reduced and cost of debt (K_d) is less than cost of equity (K_e). Thus, the Modigliani and Miller (M-M) approach, i.e. cost of capital is independent of capital structure changes does not seem to be applicable for the present study.

Table 3 shows the results of regression analysis of ACC Ltd. over the entire period of study (taking into account both pre-liberalization period and post-liberalization period) covering 31 years, i.e. 1979-80 to 2009-10. The linear multiple regression model has been applied to analyze the impact of explanatory variables on the dependent variables. Independent variables here refer to size (S_1 and S_2), leverage (L_1, L_2, L_3 and L_4), non-debt tax shields (NDTS), reserves and retained earnings to total assets (RTA), liquidity (Liq.), growth (G_1, G_2 and G_3), profitability (P_1 and P_2), collaterals (Coll.) and age whereas the overall cost of capital (K_{o1} and K_{o2}) have been taken as dependent variables for the present study. In order to analyze the impact of liberalization, dummy variable having values 0 and 1 for pre-liberalization and post-liberalization period respectively has been introduced. The following linear regression equations have been fitted for the entire period of study covering 31 years.

$$K_{o1} = \alpha+\beta_1 S_1+\beta_2 S_2+\beta_3 L_1+\beta_4 L_2+\beta_5 L_3+\beta_6 L_4+\beta_7 NDTS +\beta_8 RTA+\beta_9 LIQ.+\beta_{10} G_1+\beta_{11} G_2+\beta_{12} G_3+\beta_{13} P_1+\beta_{14} P_2+ \beta_1 COLL+\beta_{16} AGE+\beta_{17} D_t+\mu \quad ....(1)$$

$$K_{o2} = \alpha+\beta_1 S_1+\beta_2 S_2+\beta_3 L_1+\beta_4 L_2+\beta_5 L_3+\beta_6 L_4+\beta_7 NDTS +\beta_8 RTA+\beta_9 LIQ.+\beta_{10} G_1+\beta_{11} G_2+\beta_{12} G_3+\beta_{13} P_1+\beta_{14} P_2+\beta_1 COLL.+\beta_{16} AGE+\beta_{17} D_t+\mu \quad ....(2)$$

The statistical significance of regression coefficients has been tested by applying student's T-test distribution. T-test has been employed to know the significance of the coefficient of dependent variables (β_1 $\beta_{2.....n}$). The coefficient of determination (R^2) has been computed to determine the percentage variation in the dependent variable explained by independent variables. The value of R^2 lies between 0 and 1. The greater the R^2 the greater the percentage of variation of Y explained by the regression model. The significance of the regression coefficient is determined with the help of t-test. The computed t-value is compared to the theoretical value of t obtained from t-table with n-k degrees of freedom. To test the statistical significance of R^2 F-test with F-

TABLE 3

Results of Regression Analysis of ACC Ltd. from 1979-80 to 2009-10

	Coefficient (β_1) (Dependent Variable K_{o1})	Coefficient (β_2) (Dependent Variable K_{o2})
Constant	136.584	30.225
S_1	-31.595 (-0.661)	153.851 (1.061)
S_2	12.243 (0.198)	-205.073 (-1.394)
L_1		
L_2	6.557 (0.543)	15.922 (1.099)
L_3	50.676 (1.601)*	-32.959 (-0.724)
L_4	-36.352 (-1.335)	36.969 (0.753)
NDTS	-1.924 (-0.763)	-8.336 (-1.713)**
RTA	0.409 (-0.376)	2.441 (0.969)
LIQ.	-11.550 (-0.675)	26.621 (0.877)
G_1	0.280 (1.819)**	0.058 (0.272)
G_2	-0.342 (-1.401)	0.237 (0.580)
G_3	-0.007 (-1.446)*	-0.001 (-0.128)
P_1	2.968 (1.618)*	-1.524 (-0.684)
P_2	-1.800 (-0.210)	1.191 (0.556)
COLL.	-1.157 (-1.381)	1.463 (1.052)
AGE	2.040 (0.900)	2.688 (0.514)
D_t	-2.203 (-1.496)*	-0.183 (-0.064)
R^2	0.575	0.837
D-W	2.138	2.116
F-Value	1.138	2.894**

Notes: 1. Figures in Parentheses represent t-values.
2. Significance at 10%, 5% and 1% is indicated by one, two and three asterisks respectively.

Source: Compiled and Analyzed from the Basic Data Obtained from Bombay Stock Exchange Official Directory, Prowess Database (CMIE) and Annual Reports of Companies.

distribution at one, five and ten percent level of significance respectively. To check the autocorrelation, Durbin-Watson d statistics has been computed. As a rule of thumb, if d is found to be 2 in an application, one may assume that there is no first order (serial correlation) autocorrelation either positive or negative. All techniques have been applied by using SPSS 16 version on the computer.

It appears from the table that size (S_2), leverage (L_2) and age have a positive and insignificant impact upon the overall cost of capital (K_{o1}) during the study period. Size (S_1), leverage (L_4), non-debt tax shields (NDTS), reserves and retained earnings to total assets (RTA), liquidity (Liq.), growth (G_2), profitability (P_2) and collaterals (Coll.) have a negative and insignificant impact upon the overall cost of capital (K_{o1}) during the study period. Leverage (L_3) and profitability (P_1) have a positive and significant impact upon the overall cost of capital (K_{o1}) and these values turn out to be significant at the 10 percent level of significance. Growth (G_1) has positive and significant impact upon overall cost of capital (K_{o1}) and it turns out to be significant at the 5 percent level of significance. Growth (G_3) has a negative and significant impact upon the overall cost of capital (K_{o1}) and it turns out to be significant at the 10 percent level of significance. The dummy variable appears with a negative sign and it turns out to be significant at the 10 percent level of significance. The negative coefficient of dummy variable indicates a decline in the overall cost of capital (K_{o1}) during post-liberalization period as compared to pre-liberalization period. The coefficient of determination, i.e. R^2 has been estimated 0.575 percent over the study period. The Durbin-Watson statistic has been observed greater than 2 indicating that there is no auto-correlation between the residuals. The estimated equation has lower F-value and it has been observed insignificant during the study period.

It appears from the table that size (S_1), leverage (L_2 and L_4), reserves and retained earnings to total assets (RTA), liquidity (Liq.), growth (G_1 and G_2), profitability (P_2), collaterals (Coll.) and age have a positive and insignificant impact upon the overall cost of capital (K_{o2}) over the entire study period. Size (S_2), leverage (L_3), growth (G_3) and profitability (P_1) have negative and insignificant impact upon the overall cost of capital (K_{o2}) over the entire study period. Non-debt tax shields (NDTS) has a negative and significant impact upon the overall cost of capital (K_{o1}) and it turns out to be significant at the 5 percent level of significance. The dummy variable appears with a negative sign and it turns out to be insignificant over the study period. The coefficient of determination, i.e. R^2 has been estimated 0.837 percent over the study period. The Durbin-Watson statistic has been observed greater than 2 indicating that there is no auto-correlation between the residuals. The estimated equation has higher F-value significant at 5 percent level of significance. It indicates that there is at least one explanatory variable in each equation that is statistically significant in explaining variation in the dependent variable.

CONCLUSION

The present study is an attempt to analyze the impact of liberalization upon cost of capital of one of the leading top-level Indian companies in cement industry, i.e. ACC Limited. A comparative analysis of pre-liberalization and post-liberalization periods for a period of 31 years, i.e. 1979-80 to 2009-10 has been done to achieve the objective of this study. The financial data for present study have been taken from the various issues of The Bombay Stock Exchange Official Directory and published annual reports of ACC Ltd. The statistical and mathematical techniques such as ratio analysis, percentages, compound growth rates and multiple regression analysis have been used for analysis of collected data. All calculations have been done by using SPSS software package version 16 on the computer. From the above analysis, it is concluded that there is decline in cost of debt (K_{dat}) but there is an increase in the cost of equity capital (K_{e1} and K_{e2}) and overall cost of capital (K_{o1} and K_{o2}) after liberalization. Using multiple regression analysis, it has been observed that leverage (L_3), non-debt tax shields (NDTS), growth (G_1 and G_3) and profitability (P_1) are significant determinants of the overall cost of capital (K_{o1} and K_{o2}). The regression coefficients of dummy variables appear with negative signs in both the cases. This value turns out to be significant at the 5 percent level of significance with overall cost of capital (K_{o1}) as the dependent variable. It is a healthy sign as it indicates a decline in the overall cost of capital (K_{o1} and K_{o2}) of this company during post-liberalization period as compared to pre-liberalization period. The findings of this study support the traditional viewpoint of capital structure theories that with the judicious use of debt overall cost of capital (K_o) is reduced and the cost of debt (K_d) is less than the cost of equity (K_e). Thus the Modigliani and Miller (M-M) approach, i.e. cost of capital is independent of capital structure changes does not seem to be applicable for the present study.

REFERENCES

Babu and Jain, 1999. Short-term and long-term debt financing in India-an empirical study of the private corporate sector. *The Management Accountant*, 34, 2, (February).107-114.

Bandopadhay, 1997. Capital structure policy and allied issues: case study of RIL. *The Management Accountant*, 32, 6 (June).

Barber and Lyon, 1997. Detecting long-run abnormal stock returns: the empirical power and specification of test statistics. *Journal of Financial Economics*, 13, 341-72.

Barges, A. 1963. The effect of capital structure on the cost of capital. Prentice-Hall Inc, Englewood Cliffs, N.J. 100-103.

Bombay Stock Exchange: The Stock Exchange Official Directory, March 1991, October 1998.

Chari and Henry, 2004. Risk sharing and asset prices: evidence from a natural Experiment. *Journal of Finance*, 59, 1295-1324.

Danial and Makina, 2005. Stock market liberalization and the cost of capital : evidence from JSE securities exchange listed firms. Forthcoming in the *Journal of Accounting and Finance Research*, 3.2.

Eun and Janakiramanan, 1986. A model of International pricing with a constraint on the foreign equity ownership. *Journal of Finance*, 41, 897-914.

Foerster and Karolyi, 2000. The long-run performance of global equity offerings. *Journal of Financial and Quantitative Analysis*, 35, 499–528.

Goyal, V.K., 1992. Cost of capital measurement in Indian industries, Deep and Deep Publications, New Delhi, 12-31.

Henry, P.B., 2000. Stock market liberalization, economic reforms and emerging market equity prices. *Journal of Finance*, 55, 529-64.

Kaur and Malhotra, 2000. Cost of debt and cost of equity-emerging trends: a case study of TISCO. *The ICFAI Journal of Applied Finance*, 6, 3 (July).

Macwan and Gabriel, 1999. Debt equity ratio of ICICI assisted industries-an exposition. *The Management Accountant*, 29, 4 (April), 259-63.

Pandey, I.M. (2001). Financial Management (Eighth Revised Edition). Vikas Publishing House Pvt. Ltd., New Delhi, 493-535

Singh, Fulbag and Kaur, Sukhwinder (2007), "Liberalization and cost of capital-A case study of Reliance Industries Limited" Indian Journal of Commerce, *Quarterly Publication of Indian Commerce Association*, Vol. 60, No. 1, Jan.-March issue, pp. 37-55.

Vanhorne, J.C. (2002). Financial management and policy (Twelfth Edition). Pearson Education (Singapore) Pte. Ltd., Indian Branch, New Delhi, 393-401

3

Performance and Perspectives of Mergers and Acquisitions in the Indian Chemical Industry

N.M. LEEPSA

I. INTRODUCTION

Mergers and Acquisitions (M&A) have played important role in growth and development of companies by providing various benefits like economies of scale, economies of scope, entry into new market and other synergistic profits. M&A have also played a significant part in the chemical industry. Among all the industries in the manufacturing sector, the highest numbers of deals are done in the chemical industry. It signifies that companies in chemical industry consider M&A as an innovative and sustainable solution to stay ahead in market competition by getting ready access to technologies and market. The companies are considering buying out the ready built business at attractive valuations as a better option to stay ahead of their competitors rather than setting up any new business or facilities. It is therefore imperative to observe the M&A deals done between companies in the chemical industry and to know the motives behind going for the deals and post-merger performance of companies. The present study is an attempt to find out the current trends of M&A in the chemical industry in India, the objectives behind the M&A deals, success or failure of companies in mergers in chemical industry.

2. OVERVIEW OF CHEMICAL INDUSTRY

The chemical industry is changing due to globalisation, consolidation, product innovation and cost rationalisation. India is growing in production, exports in chemical industry attracting various parts of the world. Domestic players in the chemical industry are increasing foreign investment. As per the SMERA rating agency of India, India ranks twelfth position in production in the chemical industry in the world. The chemical industry is one of the fastest growing industries in India that contributes 2.8 per cent GDP to industry. The compounded annual growth rate (CAGR) of the major chemicals by the end of the 10th five year plan (2001-02 to 2006-07) is 4.69 per cent as against 5.55 per cent in its consumption during the corresponding period. The growth in import and export of the major chemical increased annually at the rate of 14.79 per cent and 14.13 per cent respectively.* The Indian Chemical Industry compromises many areas like inorganic chemicals, caustic soda, fertilizers, pesticides, paints and varnishes, dyes and pigments, drugs and pharmaceuticals, cosmetics, toiletries, soaps and detergents, soda ash, organic chemical, other chemicals, polymers, plastic products, petroleum products, tyres, tubes, rubber and rubber products. According to a recent KPMG study, the massive capacity expansion in bulk chemicals in West Asia between now and 2015 may make around one-fifth of the European petrochemical industry uncompetitive. This would result in various M&A activities globally.

The key characteristics of chemical industry demand that the chemical companies should have up to date technology and research and development (R&D) oriented facilities so as to maintain relatively high margins of profits. In general, the factors that affect the success of the chemical industry are cost competitiveness, diversified product mix for domestic as well as international market, technology capabilities; environmental and safety measure (SMERA rating agency of India). In fact, chemical industry in India is affected by costly supply chains, expensive sales organisation, lack of quality and efficiency in innovation, increasing the need for capital leading to overcapacities, erosion of prices and margins. This has led to the distinction between the Speciality and Commodity chemicals. Commodity chemicals have been established for a period of time, and many firms compete to distribute high volume. The profit margins on such chemicals are low. Specialty chemicals result

Source: *Rating criteria for different Key-Industries, http://smera.in/smera/criteria asp&lang=eru&output=json

from firm innovation and provide firms with high profit margin due to competitive advantage. However, as more firms enter the market segment, the margins will be reduced by increasing industry capability. Specialised engineering firms have aided the rapid dispersal of technology. These firms install turnkey chemical production plants, making it difficult for firms to maintain a competitive advantage based on production procedures. Thus, M&A should be made taking into account all these aspects of the chemical industry.

3. TRENDS OF MERGERS AND ACQUISITIONS IN CHEMICAL INDUSTRY

India's M&A in the chemical industry is growing at its record level in recent years. Due to the side effects economic slowdown like slow down of demand has resulted in number of M&A. The There is 1440 merger and 4694 acquisition deals done in India. The following figure shows the M&A deals in different industries of manufacturing sector:

FIGURE 1

Industry-wise M&As Deals done in India

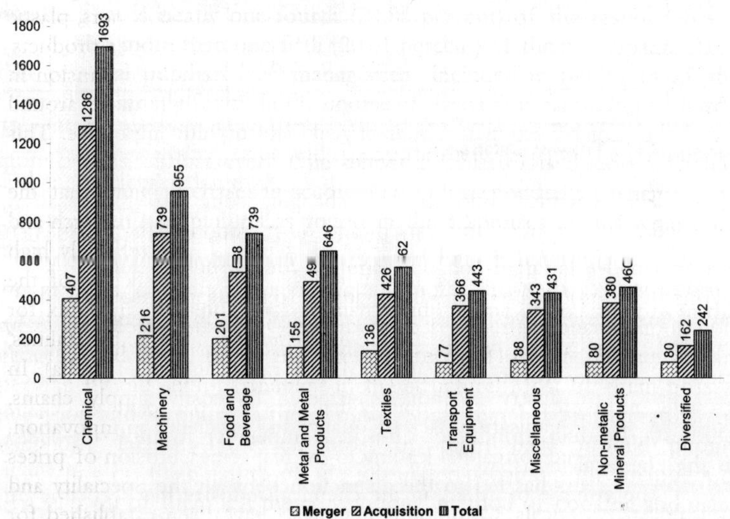

Source: CMIE Prowess Database.

If the rank of M&A deals is seen in individual industry, then highest deals are done in chemical industry followed by, machinery, food and beverage, metals & metal products, textiles. India's M&A in the chemical industry is growing at its record level in recent years. Among all the industries in the manufacturing sector, the highest numbers of deals are done in the chemical industry from 2000 to 2011. M&A in chemical industry constitutes around 28 per cent of the total deals.

TABLE I

M&A in Chemical Industries

Year	Merger	Acquisition	M&A Total
2000	38	117	155
2001	35	113	148
2002	39	109	148
2003	30	105	135
2004	39	112	151
2005	40	93	133
2006	42	116	158
2007	26	136	162
2008	28	131	159
2009	23	66	89
2010	42	65	107
2011	25	123	148
Total	**407**	**1286**	**1693**

Source: CMIE Prowess Database.

The chemical industry is changing due to globalisation, consolidation, product innovation and cost rationalisation. India is growing in production and exports in chemical industry attracting various parts of the world. Domestic players in the chemical industry are increasing foreign investment. As per the SME Rating Agency of India Limited, India ranks twelfth position in production in the chemical industry in the world. The chemical industry is one of the fastest growing industries in India that contributes 2.8 per cent of Gross Domestic Product to industry. Thus, it is imperative to know the M&A in the chemical industry.

The volume of M&A in the chemical industry has seen upward and downward trend over the period of time. From 2000 to 2001, there is fall in M&A activities in the chemical industry by five per cent and it further reduced in 2003 by nine per cent. Although there is no change in the number of M&A in chemical industry in the year 2002 but the value went up by 272 per cent compared to 2001. The year 2004 has seen a rise in the M&A activities in chemical industry both in volume (12 per cent) and value (174 per cent). There is fall in volume of M&A transactions in 2005 but rise in value by 72 per cent compared to 2004. The year 2006 saw recovery in M&A activity due to low interest rates and ready availability of cash to make deals. Due to demand reduction as the effect of economic slowdown, 2007 also saw rise in M&A activity as the M&A players consider it is better to buy a ready-made business than setting up new business to remain competitive. In 2007, M&A in chemical industry rose by three per cent in terms of volume and 115 per cent by value. These acquisitions helped in entering new markets and accessing new technologies. There is a drastic fall in M&A activity in 2009 by 44 per cent since the global financial crisis hit the market. M&A has not only fallen in terms of volume but also value in 2008 (-22 per cent) and 2009 (-73 per cent) compared to previous years. Financial market turbulence made a negative impact on all the aspects of chemical industry value chain. There is improvement in M&A activity in 2010 and 2011 both in terms of volume but in 2010 acquisition deal went up by 392 per cent while in 2011 acquisition deal value went down by 65 per cent. Around 62 companies made a series of acquisitions either in the same year or different year. It shows those who are going for any M&A deals they are doing M&A more than once in their corporate life span.

The total acquisition deal value worth is Rs. 1,63,309 crore. The largest deals are done in 2010 as the total deal value during the year was around Rs. 30,767 crore while 2001 saw smallest deal value worth Rs. 2,297 crore. The big deals in 2010 are done by reliance industries by making substantial acquisition of shares of Atlas Energy Inc (Rs. 7,550 crore), Pioneer Natural Resources Co. (Rs. 6,242 crore), Infotel Broadband Services Ltd. (Rs. 4,800 crore). Apart from this, other two in top five deals list of 2010 are Reckitt Benckiser Plc. acquiring Paras Pharmaceuticals Ltd. for Rs. 3,260 crore and Godrej Consumer Products Ltd. acquiring Megasari Makmur (Indonesia) for Rs. 1,200 crore. Although the deal value has fallen in 2008, a major acquisition deal has been made during the year namely, Daiichi Sankyo Company Ltd. acquired Ranbaxy Laboratories Ltd. for Rs. 6,819 crore.

Some of the important merger deals are Unichem Laboratories Ltd. with AVM Capital Services Pvt. Ltd. for a swap ratio of 4672.55:1 in 2011; Sree Rayalaseema Hi-Strength Hypo Ltd. with TGV Pharma Pvt. Ltd. in 2011 for swap ratio of 790:100; Kansai Nerolac Paints Ltd. with Polycoat Powders Ltd. in 2006 for swap ratio of 461:1000; Elgi Rubber Co. Ltd. with Elgi Rubber Products Ltd. in 2008 for swap ratio of 280:1; Diamines & Chemicals Ltd. with Alkyl Finance & Trading Ltd. in 2001 for swap ratio of 225:1.

The total consideration of all acquisition deals in this industry is around Rs. 1,63,309 crore. During the year 2001 many big acquisitions are made compared to other years that amounted to Rs. 30,707 crore. The top five deals of 2001 are Janus Capital Corporation of USA that acquired Reliance Industries Ltd. for Rs. 650 crore, Recon Healthcare Ltd. acquired German Remedies Ltd. for Rs. 256 crore, Buy Back of Share of Tata Chemicals Ltd. Rs. 163 Crore, Abbott UK & Abbott USA acquired Abbott India Ltd. 106 crore, International Finance Corporation acquired Orchid Chemicals & Pharmaceuticals Ltd. Rs. 97 crore. The year 2010 is not favourable for chemical industry M&A in terms of deal value since lowest deal value is seen during this year that amounted to Rs. 2,297 crore.

The following chart shows the trend of M&A deals in the chemical industry in India:

FIGURE 2

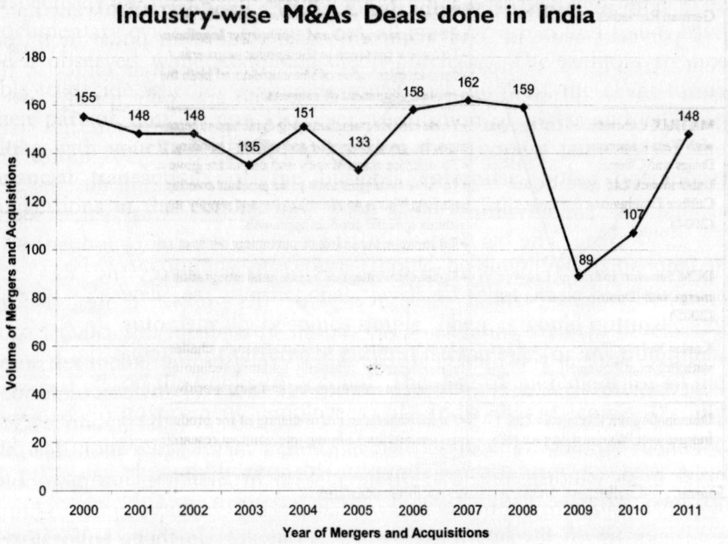

Industry-wise M&As Deals done in India

Source: CMIE Prowess Database.

4. MOTIVES OF M&AS IN CHEMICAL INDUSTRY

Some of the M&A motives of companies in the chemical industry are discussed below:

TABLE 2

M&As Motives of Chemical Industry

M&A deals	*Reasons for Merger and Acquisitions*
Hindustan Organic Chemicals Ltd. merged with Hindustan Fluoro-carbons Ltd (2000)	•To end its longstanding losses during 1995-96.
Novartis India Ltd. merged with Ciba Ckd Biochem Ltd. (2001)	•To protect from losing a secure and a quality source of refampicin as CCBL has been under the danger of becoming a sick company
Castrol India Ltd. merge withTata BP Lubricants India Ltd. (2001)	•To enhance distribution network. •To enable the company to enter the lower segment of the industry through the Tata BP brand in addition to the dominant presence in the premium segment through its Castrol brand of lubricants.
Matrix Laboratories Ltd. merged with Vorin Laboratories Ltd. and Medicorp Technologies India Ltd. (2002)	•To better utilise the capacities of the three companies by getting the economies of scale •To tap the regulated markets.
Cadila Healthcare Ltd. merged with German Remedies Ltd. (2003)	•To have strength of size, scale and integration of operations. •To have access to new product pipelines of multinational companies such as Schering AG and Boehringer Ingelheim. •To have a presence in therapeutic segments. •To maximise value of shareholders of both the companies and achieve complete alignment of interests.
MATRIX Laboratories Ltd. merged with Vera Laboratories Ltd., Fine Drugs and Chemicals Ltd.,Medikon Laboratories Ltd. (Medikon) and Calibre Engineering Pvt Ltd. (2004)	•To de-risk its manufacturing facilities in terms of manufacturing capacity, product profile and effluent handing facilities. •To enhance transparency and corporate governance practices. •To have synergies such as no product overlap and the USFDA facility entailing Matrix to manufacture and supply any additional products without specific product approvals. •To improve servicing its customers without any capacity constraints
DCM Shriram Industries Ltd. merge with Daurala Organics Ltd. (2005)	•To take advantage of operational integration and consolidation.
Kansai Nerolac Paints Ltd. merged with Polycoat Powders Ltd. (2006)	•To help companies meet increasingly challenging customer requirements by constantly updating technology, striving for greater efficiency in operations and ensuring worldwide servicing capabilities
Doctors Organic Chemicals Ltd. merged with Wanbury Ltd. (2008)	•To increase sales and widening of the product portfolio in the US markets and for foraying into contract research and manufacturing services.

Source: Collected from various online sources.

5. LITERATURE REVIEW

Mergers and acquisitions (M&As) got its significance in both developed as well as developing nations since 1990s. It has gained importance throughout the world in the current scenario due to globalisation, liberalisation, technological developments and intensely competitive business environment. The increased competition in the global market has impelled the Indian companies to go for M&A as a significant strategic alternative to survive and grow. But the question arises, do M&A really improves performance or not. Thus, deep insight into the literature has been made to find out the performance of companies involved in M&As. From the literature it is found that the performance of M&A can be examined in four different ways viz. Market Based Returns to Shareholders by Event Studies, Accounting Studies: Returns (or performance) estimated from reported financial statements, Survey of Managers, Clinical Research or Case Studies (Bruner, 2004). A study of both Indian and International research papers are made on the works relating to the post-M&A corporate financial performance.

5.1 Studies Based on Accounting Approach

Accounting based studies uses financial statements to evaluate the pre- and post-M&A performance using financial ratios. The following table shows the evidence of literature on M&A performance based on accounting approach.

TABLE 3

Studies Based on Accounting Approach

Findings	*Evidence*
Negative Returns	
There is no positive return from the merger. Return on Asset for securing firms consistently declined in post-merger years	Meeks (1977); Carline, Linn & Yadav (2001), Ghosh (2001)
The firms involved in M&A activity are less profitable, although not significantly so, than comparable firms	Mueller (1980) cited from Bruner (2004)
Both related and unrelated deals makes significant losses in market share	Mueller, 1985 cited from Bruner (2004).
The acquirer's return on assets is same as of control firms in the post-acquisition period.	Healy, Palepu, Ruback (1992)
Acquirers get two per cent lower return on assets than non-acquirers in post-acquisition.	Dickerson, Gibson & Euclid (1997)
Positive Returns	
Long-term operating performance is positive but insignificant.	Kruse *et al.* (2002)
The acquisitions lead to improvements in long-run operating cash flow performance.	Rahman & Limmack (2004).

Accounting-based studies shows mixed results.

5.2 Studies Based on Event Study Approach

The majority of takeover event studies or share return studies examine share returns to the acquirer and acquiree over a short-run period surrounding the announcement.

There is no conclusive evidence as whether M&A are value creating or value destroying activities. The studies have focused on manufacturing companies in general. Limited studies, as far literature review is concerned is made in chemical industry, more specifically few studies have been carried out in India. Therefore, the present study focuses on the financial performance of chemical companies in the post-M&A period.

TABLE 4

Studies Based on Event Study Approach

Findings	*Evidence*
Negative Returns	
Acquisitions are not value-enhancing for shareholders.	Morck *et al.* (1990)
Stockholders of the acquiring firm face significant wealth loss after merger over five years.	Agrawal *et al.* (1992)
There is a small and insignificant abnormal return for acquirer at the date of takeover announcement.	Halpern (1973); Mandelkar (1974); Ellert, (1976) from Brailsford & Knights (1998)
High tech acquisitions are value diminishing in nature.	Gao & Sudarsanam (2003)
The acquiring firm has poor operating performance after acquisi tion similar to industry counter parts.	Ken (2004)
Post merger stock price and operating performance of the merged companies are negative and even worse than the firms that did not merge.	Becker *et al.* (2008)
Positive Returns	
Stockholders of target firms earn large positive abnormal returns from tender offers.	Dodd & Ruback (1977); Moeller *et al.* (2004); Dennis & McConnell (1986); Asquith *et al.* (1983)
The cumulative abnormal return is positive for acquiring firm shareholders.	Loderer & Martin (1992); Frederikslust *et al.* (2005); Dutta & Jog (2009)
Combined returns to shareholders of acquiring firm and the target firm showed Positive cumulative abnormal returns to both firms.	Berkovitch (1993) & Bradley *et al.* (1982)
Target return, acquirer return and total returns are larger when targets have low q ratios and acquirers have high q ratios.	Servaes (1991)
The acquisition creates economic value to the target firm sharehokde	Leeth (2000)
Both acquisitions and divestitures increased shareholder wealth	Mulherin (2000)

6. RESEARCH METHODOLOGY

The study is carried out using the accounting-based method.

6.1 Objectives of Study

- To find out the profitability performance of chemical companies in post-merger years.
- To find out the liquidity performance of chemical companies in post-merger years.
- To find out the solvency performance of chemical companies in post-merger years.

6.2 Sample Description

The samples are chosen for chemical companies going for merger deals only. Initially the deals are chosen for companies that have gone for mergers either as an acquirer (merging another company) or as a target (being merged into another company) in the chemical industry. The period of study is 31st March 1997 to 31st March 2011 for the sample merger deals during 1st January 2000 to 31st December 2008. The period is chosen so that data for pre-merger three years and post-merger three years can be collected. Companies for which continuous year financial data are available are chosen. Merger deals

TABLE 5

Sample Companies for Performance Evaluation

Year	*Number of Merger Cases*	*Number of Cash Deals*	*Number of Stock Deals*
2000	11	5	6
2001	14	4	10
2002	10	3	7
2003	7	4	3
2004	6	2	4
2005	7	3	4
2006	7	3	4
2007	6	5	1
2008	3	1	2
Total	**70**	**30**	**41**

6.3 Tools and Techniques

Paired t test is used for the study to evaluate the difference in the pre-and post-merger financial performance of companies in chemical industry.

6.4 Data Sources

Data are collected from centre for monitoring Indian economy prowess data base.

7. RESULTS AND DISCUSSION OF STUDY

(T0) the merger event year and likewise (T+1) is post-merger one year (T+2) (T+3). In a similar manner (T-1) means pre-merger 1st year (T-2) means pre-merger second year and (T-3) means pre-merger third year. The abbreviations used in results are the Average of (T0) (T+1) (T+2) (T+3) for Post0123 and Average of (T0) (T-1) (T-2) (T-3) for Pre0123. In same way abbreviations subsequent years are used.

7.1 Without Industry Adjusted Returns

First, the study has been carried out only of the firms involved in mergers without any comparison with the industry results.

7.1.1 Post-merger Liquidity Performance in Chemical Industry

The liquidity performance is evaluated using current ratio[1], quick ratio[2] and net working capital ratio.[3] The results of the paired t test are given below:

TABLE 6

Pre- and Post-Merger Current Ratio Performance

Paired Differences	*Mean*	*t*	*df*[1]	*Sig. (2-tailed)*
$CR_{post0123}$-$CR_{pre0123}$	-0.42	-0.51	70	0.61
$CR_{post123}$-CR_{pre123}	-0.56	-0.51	70	0.61
CR_{post12}-CR_{pre12}	-1.28	-0.95	70	0.34
CR_{post1}-CR_{pre1}	-3.46	-1.22	70	0.22

[1]df mean degrees of freedom.

The current ratios of the chemical companies have declined in the post-merger years one year, two years average, three years average. But the decline in the current ratio is insignificant.

TABLE 7

Pre- and Post-Merger Quick Ratio Performance

Paired Differences	*Mean*	*t*	*df*	*Sig. (2-tailed)*
$QR_{post0123}$-$QR_{pre0123}$	-0.58	-0.76	70	0.45
$QR_{post123}$-QR_{pre123}	-0.78	-0.76	70	0.45
QR_{post12}-QR_{pre12}	-1.24	-0.92	70	0.36
QR_{post1}-QR_{pre1}	-3.29	-1.18	70	0.24

[1] Current Ratio (CR) is defined as sum of inventories+ receivables+ cash balance +bank balance + advance payment of expenditure whole divided by current liabilities and provisions.

[2] Quick Ratio (QR)is defined as sum of receivables +cash and bank balance divided by current liabilities and provisions.

[3] Networking Capital by Sales ratio (NWCS) is defined as Networking Capital divided by Sales.

[4] df mean degrees of freedom.

The quick ratios of the chemical companies have declined in the post-merger years one year, two years average, three years average. But the decline in the quick ratio is insignificant for each year. The quick ratios of the chemical companies have improved in the post-merger years one year, two years average; three years average even though the result is not significant.

The networking capital by sales ratio has improved in the first and second year and then reduced during the third year though the decrease is not significant. Reduction in the networking by sales in third year might be creating sales challenges for the chemical companies.

TABLE 8

Pre- and Post-Merger Networking Capital Performance

Paired Differences	*Mean*	*t*	*df*	*Sig. (2-tailed)*
$NWCS_{post0123}$-$NWCS_{pre0123}$	-4.74	-0.42	70	0.67
$NWCS_{post123}$-$NWCS_{pre123}$	-6.32	-0.42	70	0.67
$NWCS_{post12}$-$NWCS_{pre12}$	5.00	0.34	70	0.73
$NWCS_{post1}$-$NWCS_{pre1}$	10.01	0.56	70	0.58

7.1.2 *Post-Merger Solvency Performance in Chemical Industry*[4]

The solvency performance is evaluated using interest coverage ratio[5], total debt ratio[6]

TABLE 9

Pre- and Post-Merger Interest Coverage Ratio Performance

Paired Differences	*Mean*	*t*	*df*	*Sig. (2-tailed)*
$ICR_{post0123}$-$ICR_{pre0123}$	3.95	2.19	70	0.03
$ICR_{post123}$-ICR_{pre123}	5.26	2.19	70	0.03
ICR_{post12}-ICR_{pre12}	2.67	1.21	70	0.23
ICR_{post1}-ICR_{pre1}	-3.71	-0.93	70	0.36

In the post-merger first year the companies were unable to earn sufficient money to pay back the interest expenses for their debt, but in the second year and third year they have earned enough to meet their fixed expenses. The post-merger three yeasr the interest coverage ratio has increased significantly. If the outlier cases are removed then even in initial year after the merger the companies have positive results for interest coverage ratio.

The total debt ratio is positive on average of two and three years in the post-merger period. During the first year there is no difference in the performance of chemical companies in pre- and post-merger period. The results suggest that the debt burden of the chemical companies increases after they go for any merger deals.

TABLE 10

Pre- and Post-Merger Total Debt Ratio I Performance

Paired Differences	*Mean*	*t*	*df*	*Sig. (2-tailed)*
$TDR1_{post0123}$-$TDR1_{pre0123}$	0.01	0.59	70	0.56
$TDR1_{post123}$-$TDR1_{pre123}$	0.01	0.56	70	0.58
$TDR1_{post12}$-$TDR1_{pre12}$	0.01	0.57	70	0.57
$TDR1_{post1}$-$TDR1_{pre1}$	0.00	0.12	70	0.90

[1] Interest Coverage Ratio (ICR) is defined as profit before interest and taxes divided by Interest expenses

[2] Total Debt Ratio (TDR) is defined in two ways. TDR1 defined as borrowing by total assets. TDR2 is defined as borrowing+ current liabilities and provisions divided by total assets.

As per the alternative total debt ratio, the following result is found out:

TABLE 11

Pre- and Post-Merger Total Debt Ratio 2 Performance

Paired Differences	*Mean*	*t*	*df*	*Sig. (2-tailed)*
$TDR2_{post0123}$-$TDR2_{pre0123}$	0.01	0.54	70	0.59
$TDR2_{post123}$-$TDR2_{pre123}$	0.01	0.58	70	0.57
$TDR2_{post12}$-$TDR2_{pre12}$	0.01	0.42	70	0.68
$TDR2_{post1}$-$TDR2_{pre1}$	0.00	0.21	70	0.84

As per the alternative total debt ratio formula, the results show the similar pattern of performance.

7.1.3 Post-Merger Profitability Performance in Chemical Industry

The profitability is evaluated using return on capital employed[7] and return on net worth.[8]

TABLE 12

Pre- and Post-Merger Capital Employed Performance

Paired Differences	*Mean*	*t*	*df*	*Sig. (2-tailed)*
$ROCE_{post0123}$-$ROCE_{pre0123}$	-0.01	-0.80	70	0.43
$ROCE_{post123}$-$ROCE_{pre123}$	-0.01	-0.74	70	0.46
$ROCE_{post12}$-$ROCE_{pre12}$	-0.01	-0.58	70	0.56
$ROCE_{post1}$-$ROCE_{pre1}$	0.01	0.39	70	0.70

During the first year after the merger the return on capital employed has improved but other has decreased in subsequent years. The company may not able to properly utilise the resources of the combined firm specifically the target company for which from the second year onwards the ROCE is negative in the post-merger period.

TABLE 13

Pre- and Post-Merger Return on Networth Performance

Paired Differences	*Mean*	*t*	*df*	*Sig. (2-tailed)*
$RONW_{post0123}-RONW_{pre0123}$	-0.07	-0.49	70	0.62
$RONW_{post123}-RONW_{pre123}$	-0.09	-0.49	70	0.62
$RONW_{post12}-RONW_{pre12}$	0.11	1.13	70	0.26
$RONW_{post1}-RONW_{pre1}$	0.20	1.17	70	0.25

[1] Return on Capital Employed is defined as profit before interest and taxes divided by capital employed.

[2] Return on Net Worth is divided by profit after tax divided by net worth.

The return on net worth has increased one year after merge and post-merger second year. When the three year average return on net worth is seen then the performance has decreased. The return on net worth has improved in the chemical industry in the post-merger first year.

7.2 With Industry Adjusted Returns

The following results show the performance of merger involved companies in relation with the counterparts in the same industry who have not gone for any merger deals.

7.2.1 Post-Merger Liquidity Performance in Chemical Industry

TABLE 14

Industry Adjusted Pre- and Post-Merger Current Ratio Performance

Paired Differences	*Mean*	*t*	*df*	*Sig. (2-tailed)*
$CR_{post0123}-CR_{pre0123}$	-0.20	-0.24	70	0.81
$CR_{post123}-CR_{pre123}$	-0.25	-0.23	70	0.82
$CR_{post12}-CR_{pre12}$	-1.05	-0.78	70	0.44
$CR_{post1}-CR_{pre1}$	-3.29	-1.16	70	0.25

The current ratio of the firms involved in merger show negative performance over all the years though statistically insignificant. The deteriorated performance reveals the firms without any merger have a better liquidity position compared to the firms involved in mergers. The companies have to look into the level of current liabilities and have to pay them off to improve the ratio, or sell of unproductive assets that may have blocked money, or increase the current assets by raising shareholder's funds.

Table 15

Industry Adjusted Pre- and Post-Merger Quick Ratio Performance

Paired Differences	*Mean*	*t*	*df*	*Sig. (2-tailed)*
$QR_{post0123}$-$QR_{pre0123}$	-0.48	-0.62	70	0.54
$QR_{post123}$-QR_{pre123}	-0.58	-0.56	70	0.58
QR_{post12}-QR_{pre12}	-1.13	-0.84	70	0.41
QR_{post1}-QR_{pre1}	-3.21	-1.15	70	0.25

The quick ratio of the firms involved in mergers show negative performance over all the years though statistically insignificant. The industry has better ability to meet its short-term obligations with its most liquid assets compared to the chemical firms involved in mergers. This indicates the chemical companies who have gone for the merger have overestimated a company's short-term financial strength for the post-merger period.

Table 16

Industry Adjusted Pre- and Post-Merger Net Working Capital by Sales Ratio Performance

Paired Differences	*Mean*	*t*	*df*	*Sig. (2-tailed)*
$NWCS_{post0123}$-$NWCS_{pre0123}$	-3.97	-0.35	70	0.72
$NWCS_{post123}$-$NWCS_{pre123}$	-5.35	-0.36	70	0.72
$NWCS_{post12}$-$NWCS_{pre12}$	5.93	0.41	70	0.68
$NWCS_{post1}$-$NWCS_{pre1}$	10.69	0.59	70	0.56

The firms involved in the merger are operating efficiently compared to the firms not involved in merger during the first and second years after mergers. Thus M&A involved chemical firms generate shareholder's value by adopting an optimum working capital balance. But when the average of three years is taken, the sample M&A involved chemical companies fail to manage their short-term assets and thus with negative net working capital as against sales.

7.2.2 Post-Merger Solvency Performance in Chemical Industry

The interest coverage ratios of the firms involved in mergers show positive returns over all the years though which is significant in a period of three years. It indicates that the mergers have improved the paying capacity of the companies for fixed charges.

The total debt ratio 1 is high in the post-M&A period though statistically insignificant in all the relevant years. This indicates that the counterparts have better financial health and less company level risk compared to the firms involved in mergers.

Table 17

Industry-Adjusted Pre- and Post-Merger Interest Coverage Ratio Performance

Paired Differences	*Mean*	*t*	*df*	*Sig. (2-tailed)*
$ICRpost_{0123}$-$ICRpre_{0123}$	3.68	2.03	70	0.05
$ICRpost_{123}$-$ICRpre_{123}$	4.96	2.06	70	0.04
$ICRpost_{12}$-$ICRpre_{12}$	2.52	1.15	70	0.26
$ICRpost_{1}$-$ICRpre_{1}$	-3.72	-0.93	70	0.36

Table 18

Industry Adjusted Pre- and Post-Merger Total Debt Ratio 1 Industry

Paired Differences	*Mean*	*t*	*df*	*Sig. (2-tailed)*
$TDR1post_{0123}$-$TDR1pre_{0123}$	0.01	0.49	70	0.62
$TDR1post_{123}$- $TDR1pre_{123}$	0.01	0.68	70	0.50
$TDR1post_{12}$- $TDR1pre_{12}$	0.01	0.74	70	0.46
$TDR1post_{1}$- $TDR1pre_{1}$	0.00	0.19	70	0.85

Table 19

Industry Adjusted Pre- and Post-Merger Total Debt Ratio 2 Performance

Paired Differences	*Mean*	*t*	*df*	*Sig. (2-tailed)*
TDR2post0123-TDR2pre0123	0.00	-0.01	70	0.99
TDR2post123- TDR2pre123	0.00	-0.21	70	0.83
TDR2post12- TDR2pre12	0.00	-0.05	70	0.96
TDR2post1- TDR2pre1	-0.01	-0.34	70	0.74

The total debt ratio 2 is indifferent in post-merger years over all the years except in the first post-merger year where the debt burden has reduced. Chemical companies suffered from increase in debt burden compared to industrial counterparts in post-second year of the merger.

7.2.3 Post-Merger Profitability Performance in Chemical Industry

The return on capital employed is negative in the average of three years and average of four years including the event year. There is a difference in the performance of companies in the post-M&A period. This shows there is an increase in borrowing that has reduced shareholders' earnings during third year. ROCE is higher in first year post-merger than the rate at which the company borrows as indicated from the TDR, thus showing that efficiency and profitability of chemical companies' capital investments is good.

TABLE 20

Industry Adjusted Pre- and Post-Merger Return on Capital Employed Performance

Paired Differences	*Mean*	*t*	*df*	*Sig. (2-tailed)*
$ROCE_{post0123}$-$ROCE_{pre0123}$	-0.01	-0.54	70	0.59
$ROCE_{post123}$-$ROCE_{pre123}$	-0.01	-0.56	70	0.58
$ROCE_{post12}$-$ROCE_{pre12}$	0.00	-0.25	70	0.80
$ROCE_{post1}$-$ROCE_{pre1}$	0.01	0.46	70	0.65

TABLE 21

Industry Adjusted Pre- and Post-Merger Return on Networth Performance

Paired Differences	*Mean*	*t*	*df*	*Sig. (2-tailed)*
$RONW_{post0123}$-$RONW_{pre0123}$	-0.09	-0.63	70	0.53
$RONW_{post123}$-$RONW_{pre123}$	-0.11	-0.62	70	0.53
RONWpost12-RONWpre12	0.09	0.93	70	0.35
RONWpost1-RONWpre1	0.19	1.11	70	0.27

The return on net worth also does not show positive performance during the average three years. The overall efficiency of firms involved in mergers is better in the first two years after merger compared to firms not involved in merger in the same chemical industry

8. CONCLUSION

The chemical companies go for M&A for various reasons like to withstand losses, increase distribution net work, procure continuous raw material sources, tap regulated markets, and achieve economies of scale, widening product portfolio. In terms of liquidity ratio, the industry has performed better than the chemical companies involved in mergers. The ability to repay short-term creditors is negative in terms of current ratio, quick ratio and net working capital ratio. The net working capital by sales ratio is positive only for the second year. There is no statistically significant impact on the debt rations on merger performance. Using the industry adjusted return performance; the results suggest that the merger has a positive effect on interest paying capacity of chemical companies. The chemical companies also do not perform well in terms of profitability in an average of three years. However, the return on net worth was positive in the second year after the merger. There is no difference in the pre- and post-return on capital employed. There is no difference in performance of chemical companies with and without industry adjusted returns. It shows that mergers have no impact on the performance of the chemical companies. The reason may be the chemical company goes for mergers mostly for combining the R&D facilities. But R&D may be the last option to discuss during the M&A negotiation. Thus, by neglecting the key objectives of the merger, the chemical industry fails to perform well in post-merger period. The mergers and acquisitions in the chemical industry should be done taking into consideration the cost competitiveness, diversified product mix for domestic as well as international market, technology capabilities, environmental and safety measure that would be brought through M&A. The future scope of the study is to look into the post-acquisition performance of chemical companies and to look into the R&D investments and R&D cost aspects after merger and acquisitions.

Notes and References

1. Current Ratio (CR) is defined as sum of inventories+ receivables+ cash balance +bank balance + advance payment of expenditure whole divided by current liabilities and provisions.
2. Quick Ratio (QR) is defined as sum of receivables +cash and bank balance divided by current liabilities and provisions.
3. Net Working Capital by Sales ratio (NWCS) is defined as Networking Capital divided by Sales.
4. df mean degrees of freedom.
5. Interest Coverage Ratio (ICR) is defined as profit before interest and taxes divided by Interest expenses.
6. Total Debt Ratio (TDR) is defined in two ways. TDR1 defined as borrowing by total assets. TDR2 is defined as borrowing+ current liabilities and provisions divided by total assets.
7. Return on Capital Employed is defined as profit before interest and taxes divided by capital employed.
8. Return on Net Worth is divided by profit after tax divided by net worth.

REFERENCES

Asquith, P., Bruner, R.F., Mullins, D.W. (1983). The Gains to Bidding Firms from Merger, *Journal of Financial Economics*, 11(1-4), 121-39.

Becker, J. R., Goldberg, L.G., and Kaen, F.R. (2008). Mergers and Acquisitions as a Response to the Deregulation of the Electric Power Industry: Value Creation or Value Destruction?, *Journal of Regulatory Economics*, 33(1), 21-53.

Berkovitch, E. and Narayanan, M.P. (1993). Motives for Takeovers: An Empirical Investigation, *Journal and Financial Quantitative Analysis*, 28 (3), 347-62.

Brailsford, T.J. and Knights, S. (1998). The Financial and Non-Financial Effects of Corporate Takeovers, Working Paper No. 23/98, Melbourne Institute of Applied Economic and Social Research retrieved on 6th June, 2010 from http://www.melbourneinstitute.com/wp/wp1998n23.pdf

Bruner, R.F. (2004). Applied Mergers and Acquisitions, John Wiley and Sons.

Carline, N.F., Linn, S.C., and Yadav, P.K. (2004). Can the Stock Market systematically make use of Firm and Deal Specific Factors when initially Capitalising the Real Gains from Mergers and Acquisitions?, retrieved on 12th May 2009 from http://papers.ssrn.com/sol3/papers.cfm?abstract_id=567110

Dennis, D.K. and Mcconnell, J.J. (1986). Corporate Mergers and Security Returns, *Journal of Financial Economics*, 16 (2), 143-87.

Dickerson, A.P., Gibson, H.D., and Euclid (1997). The Impact of Acquisitions on Company Performance: Evidence from a Large Panel of UK Firms, *Oxford Economic Papers, New Series*, 49(3), 344-61.

Dodd, P., and Ruback, R. (1977). Tender Offers and Shareholder Returns: An Empirical Analysis, *Journal of Financial Economics*, 5 (3), 371-74.

Dutta, S., and Jog, V. (2009). The Long-Term Performance of Acquiring Firms: A Re-Examination of an Anomaly, *Journal of Banking and Finance*, 33(8), 140-41.

Express Pharma Pulse (2000). *Novartis to restructure Ciba-CKD debt*. [ONLINE] Available at: http://www.expresspharmaonline.com/20010503/corpmon2.htm. [Last Accessed 27 June 2012].

Fan, J.P.H., and Goyal, V.K. (2002). On the Patterns and Wealth Effects of Vertical Mergers, Hong Kong , *University of Science and Technology Working Paper*, retrieved on 2nd May 2010 from http://papers.ssrn.com/sol3/papers.cfm?abstract_id=296435

Fourth-Quarter 2011 Global Chemicals Mergers And Acquisitions Analysis, accessed on 23rd February 2012 available from http://www.pwc.com/en_US/us/industrial-products/assets/chemical-compounds-q4-2011.pdf

Frederikslust, R.A.I.V., and Wal, V.V.D, Westdijk, H. (2005). Shareholder Wealth Effects of Mergers and Acquisitions, retrieved on May 18, 2009 from http://www.efmaefm.org/efma2005/papers/262-van-frederikslust_paper.pdf

Gao, L. and Sudarsanam, P. S. (2003). Value Creation in UK High Technology Acquisitions, retrieved on 4th June 2009 from http://papers.ssrn.com/sol3/papers.cfm?abstract_id=493762, accessed on

Ghosh, A. (2001). Does Operating Performance really improve following Corporate Acquisitions? *Journal of Corporate Finance*, 7(2), 151-78.

Kansai Nerolac Points Ltd. accessed on 23rd Feb. 2012 available from http://www.nerolac.com/index.jsp?pagw=company/share@lang

Ken, C. Y. (2004). The Measurement of Post-Acquisition Performance using EVA, retrieved on 12th March 2010 from http://www.allbusiness.com/public-administration/administration-economic-programs/990660-1.html

Kruse, T.A., Park, H.Y., Park, K., and Suzuki, K. (2002). The Value of Corporate Diversification: Evidence from Post-Merger Performance in Japan, retrieved on 10th February 2010 from http://papers.ssrn.com/sol3/papers.cfm?abstract_id=344560

Leeth, J.D. and Borg, J. R. (2000). The Impact of Takeovers on Shareholder's Wealth during the 1920s Merger Wave, *Journal of Financial and Quantitative Analysis*, 35 (2), 217-38.

Loderer, C., and Martin, K. (1992). Post-Acquisition Performance of Acquiring Firms, *Financial Management*, 21, 69-79.

Mantravadi, P. and Reddy, A. V. (2008). Post-Merger Performance of Acquiring Firms from Different Industries in India, *International Research Journal of Finance and Economics*, 22, 192-204.

Moellera, S.B., Schlingemannb, F.P. and Stulz, R.M. (2004). Firm Size and the Gains from Acquisitions, *Journal of Financial Economics*, 73(2), 201-28.

Morck, R., Shleifer, A., and Vishny, R.W. (1990). Do Managerial Objectives Drive Bad Acquisitions?, *Journal of Finance*, 45 (1), 31-48.

Pawaskar, V. (2001). Effect of Mergers on Corporate Performance in India, *Vikalpa*, 26(1), 19-32.

Rahman, R.A., and Limmack, R.J. (2004). Corporate Acquisitions and the Operating Performance of Malaysian Companies, *Journal of Business Finance and Accounting*, 31(3-4), 359-400.

Ramaswamy K.P. and Waegelein, J.F. (2003). Firm Financial Performance following Mergers, *Review of Quantitative Finance and Accounting*, 20 (2), 115-26.

Servaes, H. (1991). Tobin's Q and the Gains from Takeovers, *Journal of Finance*, 4 (1), 409-19.

SMERA Rating Agency of India Report, Rating Criteria For Chemical Industry accessed on 23rd February 2012 available from http://www.smera.in/smera_pdf/RATING?%20CRITERIA?%20FOR?%20DIFFERENT?%20INDUSTRY/RATING?%20CRITERIA?%20FOR?%20CHEMICAL?%20INDUSTRY.pdf

Pairs' Trading

Raghu Katragadda and B. Hari Babu

INTRODUCTION

Pairs Trade or Spread Trading is a market neutral strategy that enables traders to profit through simple and relative-low risk position in the market. For over two decades Pairs trading is a popular quantitative method of statistical arbitrage that has been widely used in the financial industry.

The pair trading was pioneered by Gerry Bamberger and later led by Nunzio Tartaglia's quantitative group at Morgan Stanley in the 1980's (Vidyamurthy, 2004). Since then this short-term strategy has been of enormous interest in the quantitative speculation and a Statistical Arbitrage tool of colossal importance equally for both the hedge funds and investment bankers.

The concept of pairs trading is disarmingly simple, but can be one of the most complex types of trading in practice. Where two stocks have to be identified whose prices have moved historically; and when the spread between them widens, an undervalued stock has to be bought (long position), while the other stock which is relatively expansive/over-valued need to be sold (short position). In short, Pair trading, also known as statistical arbitrage is a market-neutral trading strategy where the goal is to match two shares that are highly correlated, trading one long and the other short.

CHOICE OF SECURITY AND MODEL CONSTRUCTION

Pair's Trade can be applied to almost any type of security, be it fixed income, convertible bonds, futures, options and, equities. Before forming a portfolio one has to follow a screening process, hence the pair's trader should consider the liquidity of the securities, the short-sale ability, corporate actions and restricted sectors. Then the trader should have an in-depth understanding of the fundamentals and technical analysis surrounding the selected stock, for example, Cipla and Ranbaxy.

Many of the technical and the fundamental principles that affect Cipla also affect Ranbaxy, but some principles are very specific to an individual type of instrument and distinct way of implementing the strategy is through the application of statistical filters are highly for the securities that highly correlated. Correlation is a statistical coefficient that measures the strength, within a range of +1 to -1, of the relationship between two variables. These factors can be estimated from the subset of the data using the following steps:

1. Arrange the data into *x*, *y* pairs, i.e. Cipla and Ranbaxy,
2. Compute the mean of all of the *x* value,
3. Compute the sum of the x^2 by squaring each value of *x* and adding the squares,
4. Compute the sum of the y^2 using the same method,
5. Compute the sum of each *x* value multiplied by its corresponding *y* value,
6. Calculate the slope (*b*) of the line as,

$$b = \frac{\Sigma X_i \ Y_i - [(\Sigma X_i) * (\Sigma Y_i)/n]}{\Sigma X_i^2 \ [(\Sigma X_i)^2]}$$

7. Calculate the y-intercept (*a*) where $x = 0$ by the following formula, $\boldsymbol{a = y - bx}$, while y-intercept into a standard linear equations format: $y = a + bx$

From the above equation, *y* represents the strategy return, less the risk-free rate, and *x* represents the market return, also less the risk-free rate. The value *b* calculated above represents the beta of the strategy; in this case, beta refers to how sensitive the strategy return is to the market return. The value *a* represents the strategy's alpha, also known as the value-added return, attributable to the strategy. Market-neutral strategies tend to have very low beta scores and be very alpha driven. This analysis also produces a correlation statistic, referred to as *r*, that describes the strength of the relationship between the two data sources (strategy return and market return). The main result of a correlation is called the *correlation coefficient* (or *r*) for Cipla and Ranbaxy using the following formula,

$$Cor\ (x,y) = Cov\ (x\ y,\ )/\sigma_x\ \sigma_y$$

For instance the correlation between Cipla and Ranbaxy is *0.83* (data point selected from 4th October 2010 to 31st May 2011, NSEINDIA) and when the selected pair's price diverges, a pairs trade is set-up as the historic correlation between the securities suggests that the prices are expected to converge at some point. Capturing this movement in price allows pair traders to book profits.

CHART I

Correlation between Cipla and Ranbaxy

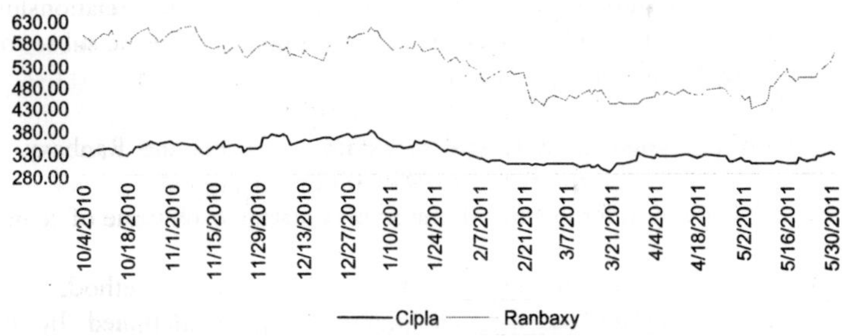

Source: from nseindia.

The simplest way is through the process of linear regression, as the method compares the returns generated by a specific strategy with the returns of an appropriately selected benchmark at the same time it helps the investor to understand the strategy of returns generation from the market swing (Douglas S. Erhman, 2006).

Security-fund mean returns stood at 0.9927,

TABLE I

Regression Statistics

Regression Statistics	
Multiple R	0.99635354
R Square	0.992720376
Adjusted R Square	0.988588145
Standard Error	43.95713994
Observations	243

TABLE 2

ANOVA

ANOVA

	df	*SS*	*MS*	*F*	*Significance F*
Regression	1	63766444.89	63766444.89	33001.47	7.6042E-260
Residual	242	467599.6967	1932.230152		
Total	243	64234044.59			

Linear regression analysis leads directly to correlation, one of the most central mathematical relationships in pairs trading, for example where we assume that x and a y represent each of our data points, then each point of the best-fit line is represented by an x and a yÄ and through application of least square method one can determine a regression line, uses the vertical deviation of each data point from the best-fit line. The sum of squares of the deviations is known as the residual sum of squares or security-fund mean returns stood at 0.9927, standard error of 43.96.

The y-intercept of the linear equation explains or represents the strategy returns, while x-represents the market returns, while the b-represents the beta of the strategy (sensitivity of strategy returns to the market returns) and 'a' represents the strategy's alpha or the value added returns.

Henceforth, while executing the pair strategy, one has to examine the historical spread between the two stocks, i.e. Cipla and Ranbaxy for a consistent correlation around the average mean. If there exist an average mean spread price and as well look for the mean Reversion point, in case of Cipla and Ranbaxy the mean Reversion *2.862* (Bloomberg). Once the pair's portfolio is constructed, one need to have an in-depth understanding on Market Neutrality

Market Neutrality

Market Neutrality is an investment strategy that has received a tremendous amount of squash over the past year and it's one of the three major features in pairs trading and a key element on which the other features of pair's trade are built. Market neutral has been one of the easiest hedge fund strategies to understand however, it is also among the most difficult to manage. As there exists distinct risks inherent in the market neutral strategies that must be properly managed in order to produce respectable risk-adjusted returns and eliminate risk.

Market neutral entrenches many different investment approaches with varying degrees of risk and neutrality, if constructed properly; market does not have an impact on the underlying results of the selected portfolio. In other words, returns generated by a market neutral portfolio are will be independent of capital market returns and provides returns in excess cash.

In short, Market Neutrality is a trading strategy that helps the investors to derive returns from the relationship between the performance of its long position and the performance of its short positions, regardless of whether this relationship is done on the security or portfolio level. Henceforth the three key features of the market neutrality strategy are *the combination of long and short investing*, the *ability to use leverage*, and the *inclusion of an arbitrage situation (relative and statistical)*.

Long and Short

For every Rs. 100 of capital invested in a typical market neutral equity portfolio, approximately Rs. 100 is held in cash, another Rs100 of stock is sold short, while Rs. 100 is held long. While the typical market neutral equity portfolio is '*cash neutral*,' this by no means implies market neutrality. In case of Cipla and Ranbaxy, on a total investment of Rs. 70,000, 100 shares of Ranbaxy are held in cash, while 156 share of Cipla sold short.

By definition, market neutrality means a portfolio has a forecasted beta, or correlation, with an equity market index of exactly zero. As a result, it has no systematic market risk. But without market risk, there are no market returns. Henceforth all returns from market neutral strategies come from one source, i.e. *stock selection* (John J. Schmitz, 2002). Without positive stock selection, or alpha, a market neutral portfolio generates a risk-free rate, less fees and expenses. The manager must be able to select stocks for the long component of the portfolio so prices rise more than the stocks selected for the short component of the portfolio in 'up' equity markets.

Arbitrage situation is the centrality for pairs trading as the strategy seeks to exploit an inefficiency in the market, whereby an investor buys a security and simultaneously sells a security for profit. "The inefficiency does exist in the market based on the investor's perception as relationship between two securities has deviated from its historical average in a statistically significant way or due to the implied pricing errors, which is the result of faulty or slow information" (Douglas S. Erhman, 2006).

The inefficiencies represent statistically significant anomalies of divergence from historically established average price relationships. In other terms, *relative-value arbitrage* is taking offsetting positions in securities that are historically or mathematically related, but taking those positions at times when a relationship is temporarily distorted. Therefore, the crucial juncture of arbitrage in pair's trade is not the divergence of prices, but the convergence of the distorted pricing of securities back to their historical levels or the Mean Reversion.

Since the inefficiencies exist, pair' trading has elements of both relative-value and statistical arbitrage, selection of pairs centers on the Mean Reversion. As one has to assume that the incongruity survive only in the short term, but that over time these anomalies will correct or mean-revert. When one stock's price anomaly reverts back to the mean price of its group, this is known as Mean Reversion.

Market Neutrality and Risk

Like any other investment strategy, Market Neutrality too comes with certain risks that are specific to this style of investing. While a good market-neutral manager may be able to reduce the level of systematic risk in his portfolio and produce superior risk-adjusted returns, he is more susceptible to other types of risk than a more traditional manager. Stock selection risks consist of idiosyncratic and systematic risk. *Model risk*, *execution risk*, and *security selection risk* are three of the most significant and should be considered before an investor decides to pursue this type of strategy.

Model risk refers to the ability of a manager's 'proprietary model' to accurately predict the price movement for which it was designed. Different fund managers place various levels of importance on their models, but most use one to a greater or lesser extent as a part of their investment process (Ganapathy Vidyamurthi, 2004). Statistical arbitrage managers, for example, rely almost exclusively on the buy and sell signals produced by their models; in many cases, complex computer systems execute trades automatically as they are generated by the model.

Execution risk can be driven by 'liquidity concerns', commission restraints, margin ability issues, and short sale rules, but in each case the concern is that poor execution will adversely affect portfolio returns. Because a market-neutral strategy invests in the relationship between stocks and then profits as their relationship converges back toward its historical average, a market-neutrality should be chosen in pious way so that one does not loose too much on spread by paying high commissions. At the same time another major concern is that even after a trade has been placed successfully, liquidity problems may make it impossible to exit the trade and realize the gain. Margin rules can affect execution but are usually taken into account before a trade is placed; they are a part of execution risk but can be managed outside of usual market effects.

On the other hand, Security selection consists of idiosyncratic risks and systematic risks that are generally random events driven by individual stock price momentum. These risks can be eliminated through diversification and, accordingly, most well-managed market neutral equity portfolios hold a large number of stocks.

Trade Execution

Once the selection and model formulation for the Pair's trade is finalized, the point of execution is initiated when the historical correlation is broken. In case of Cipla and Ranbaxy, prior to the execution, the 'average spread observed are 173.7' (Chart 2), while the 'average position of the portfolio is 1.56' towards the last trading of May'11.

CHART 2

Spread Value of Cipla and Ranbaxy

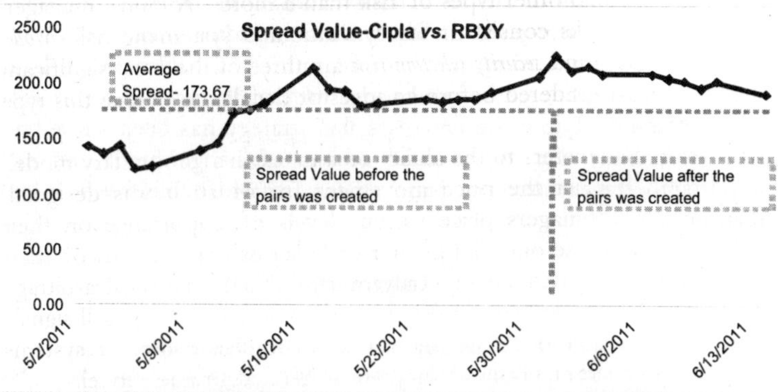

Pairs Strategy: Long 100 Shares of Ranbaxy and Short 156 Shares of Cipla—Total Investment:—70,000000						
Date	*Cipla*	*Ranbaxy*	*Spread*	*Market Neutral Portfolio*	*Spread Difference*	*Profit/Loss(on a daily basis)*
1-June-2011	327.25	538.95	211.70	1.646906035	38.03	2844
2-June-2011	325.20	541.25	216.05	1.664360394	42.38	3393.8
[illegible]	[illegible]	[illegible]	[illegible]	[illegible]	[illegible]	[illegible]
6-June-2011	331.70	540.95	209.25	1.630841121	35.58	2349.8
7-June-2011	337.60	542.45	204.85	1.606783175	31.18	1579.4
8-June-2011	334.95	537.65	202.70	1.60516495	29.03	1512.8
9-June-2011	335.60	531.95	196.35	1.585071514	22.68	841.4
10-June-2011	332.45	535.05	202.60	1.60941495	28.93	1642.8
13-June-2011	339.90	531.30	191.40	1.563106796	17.73	105.6
Profit/Loss from June 1st to June 13th, 2011						17057
% Rate of Return (assuming zero transaction costs)						24.4%

Since the historical spread had been close to distortion and execution of the pairs strategy from 1st June 2011 and reversion around 13th June 2011, the pairs trader would have pocketed a profit of Rs. 17057 (Table 3) or a 24% rate of return on Rs. 70,000 capital invested on the assumption that transaction cost is zero.

CONCLUSION

Pairs are stocks which are close substitutes according to a minimum distance criterion using a metric in price space and trading suitably formed pairs of stocks exhibits profits, which are robust to conservative estimates of transaction costs. These profits are uncorrelated any given benchmark, they do exhibit low sensitivity to the spreads between small and large stocks and between value and growth stocks in addition to the spread between high grade and intermediate grade corporate bonds and shifts in the yield curve.

In addition to risk and transactions cost, we rule out several explanations for the pairs trading profits, including mean-reversion as previously documented in the literature, unrealized bankruptcy risk, and the inability of arbitrageurs to take advantage of the profits due to short-sale constraints. During recent years this strategy has been viewed as a low profitability due to increased activity of hedge funds and more importantly the execution of pairs' strategy is not trouble-free as it looks theoretically.

REFERENCES

Gatev, Evan, William N. Goetzmann, and K. Geert Rouwenhorst, "Pair's Trading: Performance of a Relative-Value Arbitrage Rule," *Review of Financial Studies* (2006): 797-827.

Vidyamurthi, Ganapathy, *Pair's Trading: Quantitative Methods and Analysis* (New Jersey: John Wiley & Sons, Inc., 2004).

Wooldridge, Jeffercy M., *Introductory Econometrics, A Modern Approach, Third Edition* (Ohio: Thomson South-Western, 2006).

Douglas S. Ehrman, The Handbook of Pair's Trading, John Wiley & Sons, Inc., 2006.

Russell Wojcik, Pair's Trading: A professional approach, investing into future, 2004.

Daniel Herlemont, Working paper on Pair's Trading, Convergence Trading, Cointegration, 2004.

Rasmussen P.L, New approaches to statistical pair's trading by cointegration, 2005.

Layman's Guide to Pair's trading, Pairstradefinder, 2002.

Bruce I. Jacob and Kenneth N. Levy, Market Neural Strategies, edited Wiley Finance, 2005

http://www.financial-spread-betting.com/Pairs-trading.html

http://blogs.forbes.com/investor/2011/03/16/the-secret-to-finding-profit-in-pairs-trading/

http://www.investopedia.com/university/stockpicking/?partner=fdc

http://www.spreadbettrader.co.uk/pairs-trading-2.html imp

http://www.probabilityofsuccesstrading.com/?page_id=965

http://www.wilmott.com/messageview.cfm?catid=3&threadid=39044&STARTPAGE=2

http://www.seindia.com

http://economictimes.indiatimes.com/quickiearticleshow/8515366.cms

http://editorialexpress.com/cgi-bin/conference/download.cgi?db_name=QMF2004&paper_id=138

http://waxworksmath.com/Authors/N_Z/Vidyamurthy/WriteUp/weatherwax_vidyamurthy_notes.pdf

5

Auditors' Perception Regarding Vouching and Verification of Financial Transactions

RENU GUPTA AND OM PARKASH

I. INTRODUCTION

Having recorded the system of internal control and assessed its strengths and weaknesses, an auditor is in a position to plan the nature and extent of audit tests to execute in relation to accounting transactions of an organisation. An auditor adopts various procedures to obtain evidence on the basis of which he forms his opinion. One of the important audit procedures is vouching of transactions and another is verification and valuation of assets and liabilities existing in the business entity. Vouching is to substantiate an entry in the books of accounts not only with documentary evidence such as agreements, receipts, counterfoils of a receipt, contracts, but also to see that transactions have been properly authorized, recorded, and entered in the books of account.

The act of establishing accuracy and authenticity of entries in the books of account is called vouching. Verification means "proving the truth" or "confirmation". Verification is different from vouching specially in the case of assets as vouching deals with the arithmetical accuracy of accounts with regard to acquisition of assets whereas verification approves the actual existence of the assets in the entity which are appearing in the balance sheet of the company (Tandon, 2002).

Thus, while vouching, the auditor has to deal with number of cash transactions including both debit and credit side of the cash book and non-cash transactions, i.e., credit purchases, impersonal ledger, etc. In the course of examining the various transactions mentioned in the books of account with the help of documentary evidences available to him or provided to him by the client; sometimes, the auditor faces myriad of hardships in establishing the accuracy of even one single transaction. One can imagine how cumbersome the task of an auditor is when thousands of transactions take place in big business houses in one single day in spite of test checking[1] and joint audit[2]. Thus, an attempt has been made in this paper to identify the class of transactions which are found to be most difficult to be authenticated in the view of auditors participated in the study and suggest some plausible solutions in the context. The paper also aims at understanding the most appealing purpose of verifying assets and liabilities of a business firm in accordance with the participants.

After this introductory Section, the present paper has been categorised into four Sections. Section II and Section III discuss the literature review and research methodology respectively. Section IV elaborates the empirical results. Conclusions and recommendations have been mentioned in Section V.

II. LITERATURE SURVEY

Wright, Krishnamoorthy and Cohen (2002) conducted a study to analyse whether auditors are sufficiently sensitive to the type and strength of corporate governance when conducting an audit. Agrawal and Chadha (2004) examined whether certain governance mechanisms are related to the incidence of an earnings restatement by a firm. Ghosh and Kallapur (2004) investigated investor perceptions proxied by earning response coefficients (ERCs), of auditor independence-in-appearance as a function of audit and non-audit fees. Desai (2006) advanced research in internal audit (IA) evaluation by developing an IA assessment model that considers the interrelationship among the specific factors used by external auditors when evaluating the strength of the IA function. Hoitash and Hoitash (2007) provide a detailed examination of the association of audit fees with internal control problems disclosed by public companies under the provisions of Sarbanes-Oxley Act which made disclosure of internal control problems mandatory.

Krishnamoorthy, Cohen and Wright (2008) developed a case in order to alert students to the importance of non-financial information in audit process; to develop students' ability to search for relevant financial and non-financial information in the audit planning process; and to emphasise the importance of maintaining professional skepticism and to resist the natural tendency to over-rely. financial information when conducting the financial statement audit. Aurelia (2008) stated that internal audit concept is not three-dimensional irrespective of property forming the capital base, the entity organization, and the operating system-private-public-banking. Its goal is unique: to ensure the degree of control upon the operations for the entity, to guide the entity in order to improve its operations and to contribute to the adding of a plus value. Cohen, Krishnamurthy, Wright (2008) presented three alternative theoretical prospectives that help in better understanding of corporate governance: resource dependence (a strategic prospective), management hegemony (an entrenchment prospective), an institutional theory (a legitimation prospective). Bhayani (2009) states that capital market regulator, Securities and Exchange Board of India (SEBI), which was investigating insider trading charges against Satyam's promoters and some institutional investors, has widened its inquiry to cover the role of banks and the internal auditor. Murlidharan (2009) criticizes the present system of internal audit and observes that the system of appointment of auditors by a dispassionate agency in the enterprises be the ideal, but till this issue is hammered out, Murlidharan (2009, 2010) argued that dual audit may be a second solution. Gupta (2011) critically examined the definition of audit with special reference to AAS1 (SA 200) issued by ICAI. Gupta and Murthy (2012) examined the importance of internal control system in Indian enterprises.

III. RESEARCH METHODOLOGY

The present paper is carried out with the help of a structured questionnaire. A Questionnaire was sent to two hundred members of the Institute of Chartered Accountants of India (ICAI) in all which had firstly been pre-tested by ten members of ICAI. Out of two-hundred questionnaires, one hundred and sixty-eight questionnaires are returned and three questionnaires have not been included in the analysis because of incomplete responses. Thus, analysis has been made on the basis of views of one hundred and sixty-five participant auditors that constitute 82.5 percent response. The study takes into account the responses of chartered accountants who are practicing auditors only or may have experience of both auditing profession and industry. All of the respondents experience in statutory audit along with other forms of audit. Information has been collected through the internet and by post. The responses have been analyzed on the basis of simple aggregates and percentages with the help of Microsoft excel worksheet.

IV. EMPIRICAL RESULTS

IV.1 Debit Side of Cash Book

Vouching of cash book is one of the most important tasks of an auditor. After getting himself satisfied as regards to internal check for cash transactions in operation, he begins vouching with debit side of cash book that is cash receipts. The debit side of cash book includes opening balance, cash sales, receipts from debtors, income from interests and dividends, rent received, bill receivables, sales of investments, sales of fixed assets, insurance claim money, share capital issue and others. An attempt has been made in this Section to determine the most difficult item to vouch for an auditor in debit side of cash book. Responses of participants in this reference have been presented with the help of Table 1 given as below:

TABLE 1

Debit Side of Cash Book

Debit Side Items	*Number of Respondents*	*Percent*
1. Cash Sales	106	64.24
2. Debtors	36	21.82
3. Interests and Dividends	17	10.30
4. Rent Received	2	1.21
5. Any Other	4	2.43
Total	165	100.00

Table 1 states that nearly, two-thirds (64.24 percent) of the participants consider cash sales to be a most cumbersome item to be vouched. While, more than one-fifth (21.82 percent) of the respondents specify that receipts from debtors are most difficult to be examined in debit side of cash book. Whereas, interests and dividends are most difficult to be vouched as per the opinion of more than one-tenth (10.30 percent) of the respondents.

Miscellaneous transactions and miscellaneous receipts are more cumbersome to vouch as per other opinions found in the responses. On the contrary, a very few (one or two) respondents state that nothing is difficult. Thus, in accordance with the majority of participants, cash sales are most difficult to be vouched. It may be because of the fact that sales are highly adjustable in terms of trade discounts, export duties and excise duties, sales returns and so on. Furthermore, sales are subject to ups and downs due to state of economy, competition, change in technology and other various reasons which makes their evaluation difficult.

IV.2 Credit Side of Cash Book

After vouching cash receipts or debit side of cash book, an auditor is needed to examine cash payments or credit side of the book also. Some of the items appearing in the credit side of any entity are payment to creditors, wages, capital expenditure, loans, salaries, traveling allowance, bill receivables discounted, freight, insurance premium, bill payables, bank charges, partner's drawings, postages, petty cash expenses, miscellaneous expenses and bank account. An attempt has been made to determine the most difficult item to vouch in the credit side of the cash book on the basis of views of auditors participated in the analysis. Table 2 mentions the responses with respect to vouching of credit side of cash book as under:

TABLE 2

Credit Side of Cash Book

Credit Side Items	*Number of Respondents*	*Percent*
1. Creditors	30	18.18
2. Capital Expenditure	35	21.21
3. Petty Cash Expenses	91	55.15
4. Bank Transfers	8	4.85
5. Any Other	1	0.61
Total	165	100.00

Table 2 reveals that more than one-half (55.15 percent) of the chartered accountants is of the opinion that petty cash expenses are most difficult to vouch. On the other hand, more than one-fifth (21.21 percent) of the respondents consider capital expenditure to be most difficult to be examined in credit side of cash book. And nearly, one-fifth (18.18 percent) of the participants have selected creditors to be the most cumbersome item to be evaluated in cash payments.

Some of the respondents state that conveyance, tour and traveling expenses are most difficult to be examined while others consider cash purchases and cash loss is most cumbersome as found in the responses. Still, in accordance with the opinion of majority of respondents, petty cash expenses are more difficult to vouch because their number is very large and most of petty expenses are not supported by any documentary evidence such as any voucher or invoice.

IV.3 Examining Rough Cash Book

Sometimes, it is argued that the auditor is not responsible if he does not check rough cash book or diary because such books are not included in the books of account. The argument may appear to be sound to some extent but, if such books are a part of system of account books maintained by the company, the auditor will be failing in his duty if he does not compare the rough cash book or diary with the cash book. Hence, to make the picture clearer, views of respondents have further been examined in this respect. Table 3 presents the responses with regard to examination of rough cash book by the auditor as follows:

TABLE 3

Examining Rough Cash Book

Responses	*Number of Respondents*	*Percent*
1. Strongly Agree	21	12.73
2. Agree	47	28.48
3. Undecided	42	25.45
4. Disagree	45	27.27
5. Strongly Disagree	10	6.06
Total	165	100.00

Table 3 depicts that more than one-eighth (12.73 percent) of the participants are in strong support of examination of rough cash book or diary being the duty of an auditor. And more than two-fifths (41.21 percent) of the participants accept examining rough cash book as their duty in aggregate terms. But nearly, three-fifths (59.79 percent) of the respondents are either against or in a state of indecisiveness to include examination of rough cash book or diary as a part of their duty. Still, the number of respondents in favor is more than those who oppose to include examining rough cash book as part of their duty.

Thus, no clear opinion has been formed in this regard amongst the auditors participated in the analysis. Still, other than the empirical analysis as found in the responses, a very few of the respondents have commented that normally or rather generally it is not given to auditors. Another opinion is that it depends upon specific need for a specific purpose.

IV.4 Credit Purchases

Having examined the cash book, the auditor may proceed to check trading transactions. Credit purchases are examined in order to check misappropriation of goods. Some of the common ways of misappropriating the goods are inclusion of personal purchases of management in purchases of the company, wrong treatment of trade discounts availed and custom or other duty paid, missing of entries either in purchases book or in a stock book and the inclusion of fictitious or duplicate invoices as original ones. An attempt has been made to judge the most frequent occurrence while vouching credit purchases. Table 4 highlights the responses with regard to the most frequent occurrence while vouching credit purchases as follows:

TABLE 4

Credit Purchases

Misappropriations	*Number of Respondents*	*Percent*
1. Personal Purchases of Management Included in Purchases of Company	34	20.61
2. Wrong Treatment of Trade Discount Availed or Custom or Other Duties Paid	58	35.15
3. Missing of Entry either in Purchases Book or Stock Book	41	24.85
4. Inclusion of Duplicate or Fictitious Invoices as Original Ones	41	24.85
5. Any Other	1	0.61

It is indicated by Table 4 that more than one-third (35.15 percent) of the participants have found the wrong treatment of trade discount availed or custom or other duty paid most while vouching credit purchases. On the contrary, both cases of missing of entries either in purchases book or in a stock book and the inclusion of duplicate or fictitious invoices as the original ones are discovered most by equal number that is nearly one-fourth (24.85 percent) of the respondents.

Also more than one-fifth (20.61 percent) of the participants claim that personal purchases of management included in purchases of the company is mostly found in the course of evaluation of credit purchases. Thus, no strong opinion has been formed but it can be concluded that more or less, almost every type of fraud or error is discovered while checking credit purchases in accordance with respondents participated in the study. Other opinions as found in the responses in this regard are given as follows:

1. It depends upon industry and volume of transactions in the specific account head.
2. Incorrect treatment of sales and excise duty.

The conclusion is that though more or less, every type of fraud or error is prevalent but wrong treatment of trade discount availed or trade or custom duty paid is more found while vouching credit purchases.

IV.5 Impersonal Ledger

Impersonal ledger is also known as general ledger or nominal ledger. Such a ledger contains accounts from trading account and profit and loss account and adjustments related to balance sheet items. In other words, it includes transactions related to prepaid assets and outstanding liabilities, discount allowed or received, premium on share issue or redemption, deferred revenue expenditure and so on. Views of respondents have been examined to find out the most cumbersome item to be vouched in impersonal ledger. Responses of auditors participated in this respect have been categorised with the help of Table 5 as follows:

TABLE 5

Impersonal Ledger

Impersonal Ledger Items	*Number of Respondents*	*Percent*
1. Deferred Revenue Expenditure	68	41.21
2. Prepaid Assets or Outstanding Liabilities	41	24.85
3. Sales Commission	49	29.70
4. Share Premium/Discount on Share Issue	7	4.24
5. Any Other	2	1.21

It is revealed by Table 5 that more than two-fifths (41.21 percent) of the participants found vouching of deferred revenue expenditure most difficult. On the other hand, nearly, three-tenths (29.70 percent) and one-fourth (24.85 percent) of the auditors state that sales commission and prepaid assets or outstanding liabilities are more cumbersome to be vouched respectively in impersonal ledger.

Hence, though no strong opinion has emerged but it can be said that vouching of deferred revenue expenditure is most difficult. It may be due to the reason that deferred revenue expenditure belongs to several years and an auditor may be required to scan past records to check the authenticity of the transaction recorded in this respect. In the opinion of one of the participant as found in the responses, all are easy to be vouched while another claims that miscellaneous expenditure or receipt is most problematic.

IV.6 Prime Objective of Verification

Verification means "proving the truth" or "confirmation". Verification is different from vouching specially in the case of assets as vouching deals with the arithmetical accuracy of accounts with regard to the acquisition of the assets whereas verification approves the actual existence of the assets in the entity which are appearing in the balance sheet of the company. Verification and valuation of assets and liabilities involve comparing of ledger account with balance sheet, verifying the existence of assets on date of the balance sheet, satisfying that assets are free from any charge or mortgage, judging the proper value of assets, examining that assets are acquired for the business and bringing a true and fair view of business. Hence, views of respondents have been judged to determine the prime objective of verification and valuation. Opinions of participants have been classified in terms of prime objective of verification of assets and liabilities of a business firm in Table 6 as given under:

TABLE 6

Prime Objective of Verification and Valuation

Objectives	*Number of Respondents*	*Percent*
1. Comparing of Ledger Account with Balance Sheet	13	7.88
2. Verifying the Existence of Assets on Date of Balance Sheet	41	24.85
3. Satisfying that Assets are Free from any Charge or Mortgage	15	9.09
4. Judging the Proper Value of Assets	21	12.73
5. Examining that Assets are Acquired for Business	14	8.48
6. Bringing True and Fair View of Financial Statements	103	62.42
7. Any Other	1	0.61

Table 6 indicates that more than three-fifths (62.42 percent) of the participants confirm that the main objective of verification of assets and liabilities of a business firm is to bring a true and fair view of financial statements. Nearly, one-fourth (24.85 percent) of the chartered accountants are of the opinion that the checking of existence of assets on the date of the balance sheet is the prime motive behind verification and valuation. Judging the proper value of assets is also considered as the chief aim of verification of assets and liabilities by more than one eighth (12.73 percent) of the respondents.

The other opinion in this respect as found in the responses is that verification of assets and liabilities is done in order to see that disclosure of same should be made in the financial report and concept of going concern is not diluted. Thus, to give true and fair view of financial statements is the prime objective of verification of assets and liabilities in a business firm in accordance with opinion of the majority of respondents. This is because of the fact that true and fair view of financial statements is a comprehensive term and includes all other aforesaid objectives.

To summarize the empirical findings, vouching of cash sales and petty cash expenses in debit and credit side of the cash book respectively have been found to be most difficult by the participant auditors. On the other hand, checking the authenticity of the deferred revenue expenditure in impersonal ledger is more cumbersome in accordance with them. Almost, all types of errors and frauds are observed while examining credit purchases. Indifference is found in terms of examining rough cash book. And, to present the true and fair view of the financial transactions has been submitted to be the chief aim of verifying assets and liabilities as on date of the balance sheet.

V. CONCLUSION AND RECOMMENDATIONS

While conducting audit, the auditor performs distinct audit procedures; vouching and verification are two of the most important of them. He encounters difficulties while examining specific type of transactions. It can be concluded as a result of the findings of this paper that cash sales, petty cash expenses and deferred revenue expenditure in debit side of cash book, credit side of cash book and impersonal ledger respectively are most cumbersome items to be evaluated with the help of documentary evidences. More or less, all types of errors and frauds have been observed while examining credit purchases. The auditors are not able to decide whether examining rough cash book of the client forms their part of duty or not. However, verification of assets and liabilities along with vouching is done to confirm the true and fair view of the financial transactions of the business enterprise. Some operational suggestions in this context have been given as follows:

1. Accounting procedures should be simplified at national as well as international level so that task of auditors automatically becomes simple. Then, it would not make any significant difference either it is cash sales or any other item on the books of account. The date of increment for all the government employees of India has become I[st] July irrespective of their date of joining is a very good example of simplification of accounting procedures.
2. Not only some person should be made responsible for authenticity of petty cash expenses within the organization but also vendors or suppliers should be fixed for the supply or purchase of petty items and payments should be made after the expiry of a certain period of time, i.e., a fortnight, a month or so on. The organizations should ensure the applicability of the imprest system of petty cash book as well.
3. Internal check must be insured in each and every activity or transaction of the business enterprise to prevent the occurrence of errors and frauds in the business entity.

4. Specific guidelines should be framed by the authorities in relation to the checking of rough cash book of the client by the auditors whether it forms the part of their duty or not.
5. However, an undertaking is provided by the management to the auditors with regard to the true and fair view of the transactions. But, the same exercise should be done at the department level of the enterprise and hence, undertakings from all the department heads must be obtained to facilitate better internal control and overall conduct of audit.

Notes and References

1. Instead of checking all the transactions, the auditor checks only group of transactions representing all the transactions known as test checking.
2. In large business houses, more than one statutory auditor is appointed to accomplish the task in prescribed time; this system is known as joint audit.

References

Agrawal, Anup and Chadha, Sahiba, (2004), "Corporate Governance and Accounting Scandals": http://papers.ssrn.com/sol3/papers.cfm?abstract_id=595138.

Aurelia, Stefanescu, (2008), "Tridimensional Approaches of the Internal Audit: Private, Public and Banking System": http://papers.ssrn.com/sol3/papers.cfm?abstract_id =1260394.

Bhayani, Rajesh, (2009),"Satyam Scam: Banks, Internal auditors under SEBI's Scan"/ Mumbai January 16, 2009, 0:26 IST.

Cohen, Jeffrey, Krishnamoorthy Ganesh, Wright Arnie, (2008), "Form *vs.* Substance: The Implications of Auditing Practice and Research of Alternative Prospectives on Corporate Governance": http://papers.ssrn.com/sol3/papers.cfm?abstract_id =1010201.

Desai, Vikram, (2006), "An Analytical Model for External Auditor Evaluation of the Internal Audit Function Using Belief Functions": http://papers.ssrn.com/sol3/papers.cfm?abstract_id=938183.

Ghosh, Aloke and Kallapur, Sanjay, (2004), "Audit and Non-Audit Fees and Capital Market Perceptions of Auditor Independence": http://papers.ssrn.com/sol3/papers.cfm?abstract_id=612481.

Gupta, Renu and Bhanu Murthy, K.V., (2012), "Internal control System in Indian Enterprises: An Assessment", *KKIMRC International Journals—Human Resources Management*, Vol. 1, No. 2, Dec.-Feb. 2011-12.

Gupta, Renu, (2008), "Perceptions of Auditors on Various Aspects of Statutory Audit", Unpublished M. Phil. thesis submitted to University of Delhi.

Gupta, Renu, (2011), "A Critical Review of the Definition of Audit with Special Reference to AAS 1 (SA 200)": http://www.clear-research.in/CLEARIJRCM/CLEARIJRCM_pdf/chapter1.pdf.

Hoitash, Rani and Hoitash, Udi, (2007), "Internal Control Quality and Audit Pricing": http://papers.ssrn.com/sol3/papers.cfm?abstract_id=960720.

Jha, Aruna, (2009), "Auditing", Taxman Allied Services Private Limited, New Delhi.

Krishnamoorthy, Ganesh, Cohen Jeffrey, R. and Wright Arnold, (2008), "Waste is our Business, inc.: The Importance of Non-Financial Information in the Audit Planning Process": http://papers.ssrn.com/sol3/papers.cfm?abstract_id=1088444.

Murlidharan, S., (2009), "Internal Auditor from Within and Without", Business Line, Feb 12, 2009, http://www.blonnet.com/2009/02/12/stories/2009021250240900.htm.

Murlidharan, S., (2009), "Dual audit could make for a Healthy Duel", *Business Line*, February 5, 2009, http://www.blonnet.com/2009/02/05/stories/2009020550230900.htm.

Murlidharan, S., (2010), Dual Audit is a Healthy Solution, Business Line, 1 April, 2010, http://www.thehindubusinessline.com/2010/04/01/stories/2010040151000900.htm.

Tandon, B.N., (2002), "A Handbook of Practical Auditing", S. Chand & Company Limited, New Delhi.

Tandon, B.N., (2009), "A Handbook of Practical Auditing", S. Chand & Company Limited, New Delhi.

Wright, Arnie, Krishnamoorthy, Ganesh and Cohen, Jeffrey, (2002), "Corporate Governance and Auditors' Program Planning Judgments": http://papers.ssrn.com/sol3/papers.cfm?abstract_id=109317.

Investor's Perception on Different Financial Instruments

DR. B.K. SURYA PRAKASHA RAO AND B. HARI BABU

INTRODUCTION

The money we earn is partly spent and the rest saved for meeting future expenses. Instead of keeping the savings idle we may like to use savings in order to get return on it in the future. This is called Investment.

Why should one Invest?

One needs to invest to:

- Earn return on your idle resources
- Generate a specified sum of money for a specific goal in life
- Make a provision for an uncertain future

Financial Instruments

Financial instruments are transferable securities, investment coupons of mutual funds, money market instruments, options, forward contracts and similar products.

A real or virtual document representing a legal agreement involving some sort of monetary value. In today's financial marketplace, financial instruments can be classified generally as equity based, representing ownership of the asset, or debt-based, representing a loan made by an investor to the owner of the asset. Foreign exchange instruments comprise a third, unique type of instrument. Different subcategories of each instrument type exist, such as preferred share equity and common share equity, for example.

Equities

Equities are a type of security that represents the ownership in a company. Equities are traded (bought and sold) in stock markets. Alternatively, they can be purchased via the Initial Public Offering (IPO) route,, i.e. directly from the company. Investing in equities is a good long-term investment option as the returns on equities over a long time horizon are generally higher than most other investment avenues. However, along with the possibility of greater returns comes greater risk.

Mutual Funds

A mutual fund allows a group of people to pool their money together and have it professionally managed, in keeping with a predetermined investment objective. This investment avenue is popular because of its cost-efficiency, risk-diversification, professional management and sound regulation. You can invest as little as Rs. 1,000 per month in a mutual fund. There are various general and thematic mutual funds to choose from and the risk and return possibilities vary accordingly.

Bonds

Bonds are fixed income instruments which are issued for the purpose of raising capital. Both private entities, such as companies, financial institutions, and the central or state government and other government institutions use this instrument as a means of garnering funds. Bonds issued by the Government carry the lowest level of risk but could deliver fair returns.

Deposits

Investing in bank or post-office deposits is a very common way of securing surplus funds. These instruments are at the low end of the risk-return spectrum.

Cash Equivalents

These are relatively safe and highly liquid investment options. Treasury bills and money market funds are cash equivalents.

Non-financial Instruments

Real Estate

With the ever-increasing cost of land, real estate has come up as a profitable investment proposition.

Gold

The 'yellow metal' is a preferred investment option, particularly when markets are volatile. Today, beyond physical gold, a number of products which derive their value from the price of gold are available for investment. These include gold futures and gold exchange traded funds.

SCOPE OF THE STUDY

It is very much necessary for institutions offering investment instruments to study about the perception of investors towards various investment instruments because it influences the saving behavior of investors. Hence, this study attempts to know the perception of investors, understand the impact of perception on saving behavior of investors, and the factors which determine the perception of investors towards some saving instruments like Equities, Mutual funds, Bonds, Deposits, etc.

OBJECTIVES OF THE STUDY

1. To know about financial instruments which are more potential for gaining income.
2. To know about investors perception on different financial instruments.
3. To know the regulations of Securities and Exchange Board of India (SEBI) for protecting the interests of investors in securities.
4. To know the tax-saving options available to investors for different financial instruments.
5. To know how an investor can perceive in different financial instruments for getting the benefits of capital appreciation, tax benefits, risk-free return, etc.

LITERATURE REVIEW

Perception of investors about saving schemes will have a significant impact on the saving behavior of people. People with positive perception might say good things about the schemes to other people. In fact, they might act as unpaid publicity agents. Hence, it is necessary to study about the nature of perception that exists among investors about saving schemes and institutions offering such instruments.

Attitudes of investors were highly positive and showed their intention to save for a better future. Nearly two-thirds of the investors were satisfied with their savings. Both income and expenses of a family influenced the level of satisfaction over savings. Among the dissatisfied investors, the majority was of the opinion that the cost of living was too high. The most common mode of investment was bank deposits. However, a shift was noticed from bank deposits to other forms of investment. Among several parameters in investing, safety of money was considered to be the most important element. Next, the investors expected regular return from their investments.

Securities and Exchange Board of India (SEBI) and NCAER (2000) 'Survey of Indian Investors' has reported that safety and liquidity were the primary considerations which determined the choice of an asset. Ranked by an ascending order of risk perception fixed deposit accounts in bank were considered very safe, followed by gold, fixed deposits of non-government companies, mutual funds, equity shares, and debentures. Households' preference for instruments in which they commonly invested matched the risk perception. Bank deposits, which had an appeal across all income classes, and tax-saving schemes were preferred by middle-income and higher-income groups. There was a correlation between the income levels and investments of households in market-related securities.

National Council of Applied Economic Research (NCAER) (1961) 'Urban Saving Survey' noticed that irrespective of occupation followed and educational level and age attained, households in each group thought saving for the future was desirable. It was found that desire to make provision for emergencies was a very important motive for saving and importance was given next to 'saving for old age'. Among motives for saving, provision for emergencies, old age, and purchase of a house occur with the same frequencies in all occupational and educational groups.

ROLE OF SECURITIES AND EXCHANGE BOARD OF INDIA (SEBI)

The Securities and Exchange Board of India (SEBI) is the regulatory authority in India established under Section 3 of SEBI Act, 1992. The Act provides for establishment of Securities and Exchange Board of India (SEBI) with statutory powers for (a) protecting the interests of investors in securities, (b) promoting the development of the securities market, and (c) regulating the securities market. Its regulatory jurisdiction extends over corporate in the issuance of capital and transfer of securities, in addition to all intermediaries and persons associated with securities market. SEBI has been obligated to perform the aforesaid functions by such measures as it thinks fit. In particular, it has powers for:

- Regulating the business in stock exchanges and any other securities markets.
- Registering and regulating the working of stock brokers, sub-brokers, etc.
- Promoting and regulating self-regulatory organizations.
- Prohibiting fraudulent and unfair trade practices.
- Calling for information from, undertaking inspection, conducting inquiries and audits of the stock exchanges, intermediaries, self-regulatory organizations, mutual funds and other persons associated with the securities market.

Investor's Perception

Before deciding on any form of saving and investment the investor has the following perceptions:

- Set investment goals in accordance with your financial position;
- Define subjective attitude towards risk;
- Obtain as much information on the providers as possible, including past performance results and investor experience;
- Obtain as much information as possible on investment possibilities (securities and financial instruments you wish to buy), including information on potential risks; and
- Demand written information and certificates from the providers.

Before making any investment, an investor must ensure to:

- Obtain written documents explaining the investment;
- Read and understand such documents;
- Verify the legitimacy of the investment;
- Find out the costs and benefits associated with the investment;
- Assess the risk-return profile of the investment;
- Know the liquidity and safety aspects of the investment;
- Ascertain if it is appropriate for your specific goals;
- Compare these details with other investment opportunities available;
- Examine if it fits in with other investments you are considering or you have already made;

- Deal only through an authorised intermediary;
- Seek all clarifications about the intermediary and the investment; and
- Explore the options available to you if something were to go wrong, and then, if satisfied, make the investment.

Major Perception of Investor on Tax-saving Instruments

The following are some of the tax-saving options available to investors:

(1) Public Provident Fund

Public Provident Fund, or PPF, is a long-term, statutory scheme of the Government of India. Currently, the interest rate offered through government-backed small savings scheme is around 8%, which is compounded annually. On maturity, you pay absolutely no tax under Section 80C.

This long-term scheme is for 15 years; hence if your investment horizon is short-term in nature, PPF is not meant for you as it locks your liquidity for a relatively long period of time. In this scheme, you need to invest a minimum deposit of Rs. 500 and upto a maximum of Rs. 70,000 in a financial.

(2) Unit-linked Insurance Plans

Unit-linked Insurance Plans (ULIPs), which are eligible for Section 80C tax rebate, are investment products that provide the dual benefits of life insurance and savings element as a one stop solution for an individual's financial goal. However, if you don't need insurance, going with ULIP is not the best investment bet on the horizon.

Recently, insurance regulator IRDA had initiated a few corrective measures by hiking the threshold limit for ULIPs from 3 years to 5 years of lock-in period and mandated a minimum guarantee for such plans. Now, the policyholders can also opt for pre-mature exit without any penalty.

(3) Equity-linked Savings Scheme

Equity-linked Savings Scheme (ELSS) is mutual funds that help you save taxes under Section 80C as well as generate decent long-term returns from the equity markets. Such schemes are typically characterized by a three-year lock-in period.

However, the tax benefits of ELSS will be phased out with the introduction of the Direct Tax Code (DTC) starting from April 1, 2012. But, the revised code mandates that existing ELSS funds will be able to claim tax-exemptions. So, this might just be your last opportunity to put money is lucrative tax-saving mutual funds.

(4) 5-Year Bank Fixed Deposits

You might be thinking how come bank fixed deposits are included in tax-saving schemes? Since 2006, Bank Term Deposits which are of over 5 years tenure and upto Rs. 1 lakh are allowed exemption under Section 80C of the Income Tax Act, 1961. Such deposits should necessarily be in the RBI mentioned list of Scheduled Banks.

Most of such tax-saving fixed deposit avenues are of fixed tenure and do not allow pre-mature withdrawal facility. Further, such term deposits cannot be pledged to secure a loan. Most importantly, the biggest drawback of this scheme is that the interest for the amount deposited is taxable.

(5) Employee's Provident Fund

Salaried individuals are compulsorily required to contribute 12% of the sum of basic pay and dearness allowance to the Employee's Provident Fund (EPF). This sum is deducted by the employers from the monthly payroll of employees as a social security scheme akin to a forced-saving towards retirement planning.

EPF brings with it key benefits as a fixed-income instrument providing tax benefits under Section 80C at the time of investment. Even the returns from EPF are tax free on maturity. The employer also has to make a matching contribution to the EPF.

(6) National Savings Certificate

The 8% returns from National Savings Certificate (NSC) are not only assured and tax exempt under Section 80C, but also government guaranteed. Unlike PPF, NSCs have no upper limit on the maximum amount that can be invested in a fiscal year.

This small saving scheme offers tax-free initial deposit for 6 years. However, interest in NSC is taxable. But, the interest for the first 5 years is eligible for a deduction as NSC is a cumulative scheme—where the interest is reinvested and is qualified under fresh deduction in NSC.

(7) Infrastructure Bonds

In the Union Budget 2010, Finance Minister Pranab Mukherjee proposed the deduction for funds flowing in long-term infrastructure bonds in India upto Rs. 20,000 under Section 80 CCF of the IT Act, 1961.

These bonds issued by RBI-notified entities carry long tenures of 5-10 years of facilitating investment in infrastructure projects within the country. The interest earned can vary from 7.5% to 8.5% depending upon the issuer and investment option chosen. For the investors at the highest tax bracket, such investments can bring in savings of upto around Rs. 6000.

(8) Insurance

You can claim tax benefits for the health insurance premiums to the extent of Rs. 15000 under Section 80D. Moreover, you can also claim an equal amount of deduction for buying medical policies for your parents. Any amount paid towards life insurance premium for yourself or your family is eligible for tax break under Section 80C.

If you're paying tuition fees for your children's full-time education, you are eligible for tax deduction under Section 80C. Mind you, the said tax benefit is not for the donations paid to such institutions.

A CASE STUDY

Warren Buffet—An investor turns money-lender

Being a big investor in the world, he knows practically all leading Investment Bankers, banks and brokers. A first mistake every investor makes is to accept the advice of his broker or investment banker on face value. Most investors *do not* buy the stocks, but the words of the advising broker. If you want to buy say stock A (say IFCI in India) for sheer value, but your broker advises you to buy stock B (say, ICICI in India), you will buy the stock B. In short, you did not buy the Stock B but the word of your broker. If you buy some unknown stock at the instance of a broker, you are buying that broker's confidence. That is, you bought broker's word, not the stock.

It is the brokers who make the markets. They induce the enthusiasm in certain counters by active market making and increasing volume. The invitations are then sent out in the form of Broker's research, overweighting or underweighting, future projections and showing you the moon at times. Why the markets are in bad shape today? Because most of the leading brokers or investment banks have gone bankrupt or are nearly bankrupt—Bear Stearns, Bank of America, Citigroup, JPMC, Lehman, Merrill, Goldman, Morgan Stanley, UBS, RBS, Barclays, etc. The list is unending. They have no capital to make the markets or engage in pre-emptive proprietary trading. The rules are simple—If there are no brokers, there is no market.

God usually gives two chances. A person suffers two heart attacks and survives. The third is a fatal one. We as human also give two chances to wrong doer. If he errs third time, we admonish, punish, sever the relationship or dump the errand boy. Warren Buffet made the third error by investing into GS and GE.

An Investor like ***Warren Buffet*** used to have great patience in his younger days. He would wait for extraordinary opportunity, no matter how long he had to wait. It was more like a hunter that waits in the bushes to trap the tiger. It was more like Chairman Mao of China's philosophy or policy of winning a war—"Withdraw yourself from

	Warren Buffet's Gamble in Investment **Goldman Sachs and General Electric**				
	Details /Type	*His Unsecured Investment*		*Solution: Secured Investment*	
		Goldman Sachs	*General Elec*	*Goldman Sachs*	*General Elec*
1.	Date of Issue/Deal				
2.	Amount Invested	$ 5 Billions	$ 3 Billions	$ 5 Billions	$ 3 Billions
3.	Route adopted	Preference shares	Preference shares	Convertible Bond	Convertible Bond
4.	Maturity of Instrument	Perpetual	Perpetual	Limited period	Limited period
5.	Considered as	Unsecured	Unsecured	Fully Secured	Fully Secured
6.	Liquidity of Instrument	Less than 20%	Less than 20%	100%	100%
7.	Possible Premium or discount in Secondary Market	-10% to -50%	-10% to -50%	+ 30% to 300%	+ 30% to 300%
8.	Preference in liquidation	Last	Last	First	First
9.	Coupon	10%	10%	10%	10%
10.	Other Attached Instrument	Convertible Warrant	Convertible Warrant	Bonds already Convertible	Bonds already Convertible
11.	Conversion Price	$115 - Fixed	$22.25 - Fixed	$115 Variable or 20% below MP at any time	$22.25 - Variable or 20% below MP at any time
12.	Conversion Period	Not known First 5 years?	First 5 years	During life of the Bond	During life of the Bond
13.	Buy Back option for Issuer (Callable)	Yes, at any time @ 10% premium	Yes, after 3 years @10% premium	None	None
14.	Overall Security	Least	Least	Most	Most
15.	Overall Return	10% Interest 10% Premium ? Capital Appreciation		10%	
16.	Overall Attractiveness	Least	Least	Best	Best

everywhere as much deeper as you can, and let the enemy come in. When the enemy is deeply entrenched into your territory, then only pounce on him." In investment parlance, Chairman Mao would have said, "Withdraw your investments from everywhere; let the stocks or markets recede as deep as they can into your territory (buying range); then only grab them on *your terms*. However, advancing age is taking toll on him. He is now 78. He had not had luxury waiting for too long. His patience was wearing thin. And that forced him into errors. By his own analogy, he did not wait long enough at the beach to let the tide recede to see who was swimming naked. Instead he reached out few steps into the sea to grab the swimmers who would have otherwise drowned to death.

In short, he did not wait for massive return. He was enticed by 10% yield on Preference shares. Instead of being a hunter, he became hunted. He lent $ 8 billion just to earn 10% yield when the dictated FED rates were only 0.5%. He never asked himself why such blue chip companies like Goldman Sachs or General Electric should pay 10%

when the borrowings from FED could be had at less than 1%. In fact, he became a "Moneylender" from being an investor for most of his life. This was the biggest casualty of the credit crisis. Let us see how he invested insecurely and he could have invested with full security of his massive investment, nearly 25% of his Net Worth.

CONCLUSION

As a goal of getting maximum returns on investments, every investor selects as best financial instrument. All financial instruments have some sort of risk and return. Investor's main perception of instruments those having the benefit of capital appreciation, tax benefits, risk-free return, etc.

REFERENCES

Sirota Consulting, *Investment Community Interest in Reporting the Fair Values of Financial Instruments in Financial Statements—A Focus Group Summary: Final Report*, June 3, 1998.

Frederic, S. Mishkin and Stanley, G. Eakins, *Financial Markets and Institutions*, Pearson Prentice Hall, 2009.

Pathak, V. Bharati, "The Indian Financial System (Markets, Institutions and Services)", Pearson Education, 2nd ed.

De Bondt, Werner, F.M., "Betting on trends: Intuitive forecasts of financial risk and return", *International Journal of Forecasting*, 9, No. 3 (1993): 355.

Kahneman, D. and Riepe, M.W., "Aspects of investor psychology", *Journal of Portfolio Management*, (Summer 1998):52-65.

Olsen, Robert (1997b), "Investment Risk: The Experts Perspective", *Financial Analysts Journal*, Vol. 53, March/April, pp. 62-66.

http://www.financeindia.org/fdatabase.htm

http://www.yudu.com

http://www.scribd.com/doc/11538063/Warren-Buffet-An-Investor-Turns-Moneylender

http://business.gov.in/business_financing/capital_market.php

http://www.freepatentsonline.com/article/Paradigm/238426580.html

Corporate Governance: Issues and Opportunities for Financial Risk Management

MINAKETAN DASH AND SASIKANTA TRIPATHY

1. INTRODUCTION

India is on a rapid economic growth path with last three years' average rates being 9 percent and future projections for the next 5 years' being targeted at an average 10 percent. Overall there have been improved corporate earnings. The banking industry has traditionally been one of the most regulated ones in India. However, with opening up of the economy in most sectors, 1991 onwards, this industry has been no exception and has experienced a gradual phased deregulation. Several reforms have been initiated in this sector ranging from interest rate liberalization to restructuring of the public sector banks to increased competition and hence efficiency. Banks today are expected to exhibit more discipline. In tune with this, the banking sector in India has undergone structural changes during the last decade. While previously there were mostly public sector banks (PSBs) providing vanilla-type plain services, today the sector is thriving with private banks, foreign banks and PSBs fighting it out in the streets with innovative approaches and services. To complete the competitive scenario, almost all global investment banks, hedge funds and private equity firms have been reaching out to corporate customers for investment funding. So as we have already faced a crisis regarding this type of mismanagement in the banking sector also its return, we should not give that scope of management in corporate.

1.1 Objective of Study

The objectives of the present study are to find out:

1. Review about the concept of corporate governance.
2. To know about its nature and characteristics.
3. What are the issues and opportunities for present corporate.
4. Importance of Corporate Governance in banking scenario and its reforms.
5. The implementation of Corporate Governance in banking sector.

1.2 Methodology of Study

This paper is based on a literature aspect of corporate governance, its nature as well as its issues and opportunities for corporate partially and for banking sector broadly. Also the author has discussed about its effectiveness in the mitigation of risk in the banking sector by highlighting some banking reforms as the evolution of traditional corporate governance. This paper is a descriptive study and it sources of data are secondary sources like journals, magazine, articles and newspaper and publication.

2. REVIEW OF CONCEPT

Corporate governance is about ethical conduct in business. Ethics is concerned with the code of values and principles that enables a person to choose between right and wrong, and therefore, select from alternative courses of action. Further, ethical dilemmas arise from conflicting interests of the parties involved. In this regard, managers make decisions based on a set of principles influenced by the values, context and culture of the organization. Ethical leadership is good for business as the organization is seen to conduct its business in line with the expectations of all stakeholders. What constitutes good Corporate Governance will evolve with the changing circumstances of a company and must be tailored to meet these circumstances (OECD). There is therefore no one single model of Corporate Governance. "Corporate Governance is the system by which companies are directed and managed. It influences how the objectives of the company are set and achieved, how risk is monitored and assessed and how performance is optimized. Sound Corporate Governance is therefore critical to enhance and retain investors' trust." (Cadbury Report, 1992).

3. ISSUES FOR CORPORATE GOVERNANCE

These are the issues or challenges arising in the business at the time of practicing corporate governance—

- Failures in board of member in taking decisions and to understand the risk the firm is going to take.
- Conflicts between executive director and non executive director and senior executives at the time of decision-making.
- Internal and external audit failure due to negligence or less support of executive member.
- Lack of transparency of business activity due to improper transaction and organizational structure which leads to less discloserment.
- The last not the least is the corporate culture which fosters unethical behavior and encourage unethical activity.

3.1 Different Aspects of Corporate Governance

- Transparency (CSR).
- Stakeholder participation (Economical growth).
- Organizational participation (Sustainable Development).
- Accountability (Environmental & Social Responsibility).

4. OPPORTUNITIES OF GOOD CORPORATE GOVERNANCE

Substantial development of robust regulatory structure and the rules of law. A strong sustainable economy with an ability to make a long-term change. A willingness to embrace change at governmental as well as business level. Enhance good financial system and sustained financial market. Long-term benefits to the business and the economy and its comparative advantage. At the end we can say it will help the business to run in such a manner that the sustainable economic development can possible which is the main indicator of sustainable development.

5. IMPORTANCE OF CORPORATE GOVERNANCE IN BANKING SECTOR

The corporate governance of banks in developing economies is important for several reasons. First, banks have an overwhelmingly dominant position in developing-economy financial systems, and are extremely important engines of economic growth. Second, as financial markets are usually underdeveloped, banks in developing economies are typically the most important source of finance for the majority of firms,. Third, as well as providing a generally accepted means of payment, banks in developing countries are usually the main depository for the economy's savings. Fourth, many developing economies recently liberalised their banking systems through privatization/disinvestments and reducing the role of economic regulation. Consequently, managers of the banks in these economies have obtained greater freedom in how they run their banks. In particular, the nature of the banking firm is such that regulation is necessary to protect depositors as well as the overall financial system. Using this insight, we examine the corporate governance of banks in developing economies in the context of ongoing banking reforms. We discuss the changing role of government in developing-economy banking systems and the consequences for corporate governances. The special nature of banking means that it is more appropriate to adopt the broader view of corporate governance for banks as well as the government intervention in order to restrain the behavior of bank management.

5.1 Scope of Corporate Governance in Banks

- Discloser requirement.
- Listing rules requirement.
- Monitoring and enforcement.
- Proper regulator interference like RBI, SEBI and government rules and regulations.
- Transparency in business activity to its stakeholders and proper audit system to analyze the financial statement as per the S&P norms.
- Because operational activity is the main responsibility of banking business.

5.2 Issues in Practicing Corporate Governance in Banks in Managing Risk

In many developing economies, the issue of bank corporate governance is complicated by the extensive political intervention in the operation of the banking system. The pertinent issues that we briefly want to examine are government ownership of banks, distributional cartels, and restrictions on foreign bank entry. Government ownership of banks is a common feature in many developing economies. The reasons for such ownership may include solving the severe informational problems inherent in developing financial systems, aiding the development process or supporting vested interests and distributional cartels. With a government-owned bank, the severity of the conflict between depositors and managers very much depends upon the credibility of the government. However, given a credible government and political stability, there will be little conflict as the government ultimately guarantees deposits.

Risk management is the key issue in practicing corporate governance in the banking sector. The identifiable risk that is operational risk which can be properly managed by proper practice of corporate governance policy that we can conclude by focusing on the scope of corporate governance like disclosement, Transparency, governmental rules and different regulatory authority like RBI. We can detect the operational risk like—

- Cash management risk.
- Liquidity risk.
- Interest risk.
- Portfolio risk.
- NPA management risk.
- Credit risk.

All these type of risk can be mitigated by proper risk management tools, but to implement this tool corporate governance is most necessary as the board member as well as the management staff like the executives and non-executive staff will practice it in practical way. Also the cash management risk is totally depending on the bank regarding its financial status which can be studied by proper examination of financial statements.

The global financial crisis has revealed widespread and massive failures in risk management practices. Many economists, organizations and governments have suggested a link between poor risk management and corporate failings. The OECD acknowledged that although rating agencies, disclosure and accounting standards played a role in causing the credit crisis, the best boards used their own powers to overcome weaknesses and associated risks in these areas. Effective boards implemented systems which led to the efficient sharing of information and open dialogue across management and the board.

6. REFORMS IN CORPORATE GOVERNANCE

Reserve Bank of India has taken various steps furthering corporate governance in the Indian Banking System. These can broadly be classified into the following three categories: (a) Transparency, (b) Off-site surveillance, ans (c) Prompt corrective action Transparency and disclosure standards are also important constituents of a sound corporate governance mechanism. Transparency and accounting standards in India have been enhanced to align with international best practices. However, there are many gaps in the disclosures in India *vis-à-vis* the international standards, particularly in the area of risk management strategies and risk parameters, risk concentrations, performance measures, component of the capital structure, etc. Hence, the disclosure standards need to be further broad-based in consonance with improvements in the capability of market players to analyze the information objectively. The off-site surveillance mechanism is also active in monitoring the movement of assets, its impact on capital adequacy and overall efficiency and adequacy of managerial practices in banks. RBI also brings out the periodic data on "Peer Group Comparison" on critical ratios to maintain peer pressure for better performance and governance. Prompt corrective action has been adopted by RBI as a part of core principles for effective banking supervision. As against a single trigger point based on capita adequacy normally adopted by many countries, Reserve Bank in keeping with Indian conditions have set two more trigger points namely, Non-Performing Assets (NPA) and Return on Assets (ROA) as proxies for asset quality and profitability. These trigger points will enable the intervention of regulator through a set of mandatory action to stem further deterioration in the health of banks showing signs of weakness.

7. CORPORATE GOVERNANCE AS A SOCIAL RESPONSIBILITY

CSR discourse advances a concept of business responsibility at odds with traditional notions of corporate governance. Corporate legitimacy is judged on the basis of the capacities of a company to increase equity value—a capacity that is secured by the appropriate distribution of rights and responsibilities between shareholder, board, and director—the concept of CSR sets out a broader notion of goals and of the means to attain them. Both views, narrow and broad, are recognised by the companies themselves. Thus, in their statement of *General Business Principles*, declares that "We commit to contribute to sustainable development. This requires balancing short and long-term interests and integrating economic, environmental and social considerations into business decision-making".

8. FINDINGS

The major findings of the paper are:

1. Lay solid foundations for management and oversight—Recognize and publish the respective roles and responsibilities of board and management.

2. Structure the board to add value—Have a board of an effective composition, size and commitment to adequately discharge its responsibilities and duties.
3. Promote ethical and responsible decision-making—Actively promote ethical and responsible decision-making.
4. Safeguard integrity in financial reporting—Have a structure to independently verify and safeguard the integrity of the company's financial reporting.
5. Make timely and balanced disclosure—Promote timely and balanced disclosure of all material matters concerning the company.
6. Respect the rights of shareholders—Respect the rights of shareholders and facilitate the effective exercise of those rights.
7. Recognize and manage risk—Establish a sound system of risk oversight and management and internal control.
8. Encourage enhanced performance—Fairly review and actively encourage enhanced board and management effectiveness.
9. Remunerate fairly and responsibly—Ensure that the level and composition of remuneration is sufficient and reasonable and that its relationship to corporate and individual performance is defined.
10. Recognize the legitimate interests of stakeholders—Recognize legal and other obligations to all legitimate stakeholders.
11. Corporate Governance Rating be made mandatory for listed companies.

9. CONCLUSION

This paper has argued that the special nature of banking institutions necessitates a broad view of corporate governance where regulation of banking activities is required to protect depositors. In developed economies, protection of depositors in a deregulated environment is typically provided by a system of prudential regulation, but in developing economies such protection is undermined by the lack of well-trained supervisors, inadequate disclosure requirements, the cost of raising bank capital. So corporate governance is not playing a risk management tool but also it is encouraging the economical activity for economical growth which most needed for sustainable development keeping social and environmental responsibility in eyes as these are the long-term requirement for sustainability.

References

Books

Velasquez, M.G., *"Business Ethics, Concepts and Cases"*, Pearson Publication, 5th Edition, 2006. pp. 86-157.

Journal

Reddy, Y.R.K. (2009), Corporate Governance—Directions for the Next Decade, *The Indian Journal of Management*, Vol. 2, Issue 2, July-December, 2009, pp. 1-3.

Bhalla, R. (2013), CSR and Reporting by Selected Indian Companies: An Exploration, "Prabandhan", *The Indian Journal of Management*, Vol. 6, No. 1, pp. 40-48.

Articles

Heremans, D. (2007), "Corporate Governance Issues for Banks. A Financial Stability Perspective", Centre for Economic Studies, pp. 9-11.

Adams, R. and Mehran, H. (2003), Is Corporate Governance Different for Bank Holding Companies?, *Economic Policy Review*, Vol. 6, No. 1, pp. 123-42.

Arun, T.G., Turner, J.D. (2004), "Corporate Governance of Banks in Developing Economies: Concepts and Issues", *Corporate Governance: An International Review*, Vol. 12, No. 3, pp. 371-77.

Porta, R.L., Silanes, F.L., and Shleifer, A. (1999), "Corporate Ownership Around the World", *The Journal of Finance*, Vol. LIX, No. 2, pp. 471-517.

Website

Mason, M., Mahony, J.O. (2007), Governance and Sustainability Working Paper Series, Accessed on 20th Nov. 2012 from http://eprints.lse.ac.uk/3762/1/Post-traditional_corporate_governance.pdf

A Study of Microfinance Risks in the Current Scenario

Shalini Srivastava

INTRODUCTION

Microfinance refers to small scale financial services including both credits and deposits provided to people who farm or fish or herd, operate small or microenterprises where goods are produced, recycled, repaired and treated; provide services; work for wages or commissions; gain income from renting out small amounts of land, vehicles, draft animals, machinery and tools; in both rural and urban areas.

Microfinance in India has evolved in early 1980's with an effort of forming (Small Help Group) to provide access to financial services to needy.

India is second most populous country with a large number of unfinanced poor people.

There were more than 69.53 lakh savings-linked SHG and more than 48.51 lakh credit-linked SHG covering 9.7 crore poor households, as on 31 March 2010, under the microfinance programme.

MAIN FEATURES OF MICROFINANCE

Lend to the Poor	Do not take security	Prefer saving over borrowings	Small short-term loans	Cost covering interest rates	Group appraisal and guarantee	Prefer women customers over men

CATEGORIES OF MICROFINANCE RISK

There are five main categories of Microfinance risk:

- Financial Risk
- Operational Risk
- Strategic Risk
- Institutional Risks
- External Risks

Financial Risk

- Credit Risk is the risk to earnings or capital due to borrowers' late and non-payment of loan obligations.
- Credit Risk includes both transaction risk and portfolio risk.
- Transaction Risk refers to the risk in individual loans.
- Portfolio Risk refers to the risk inherent in the composition of the overall loan portfolio.
- Liquidity Risk is the risk that an MFI cannot meet its obligations on time.
- Market Risk includes interest rate risk, foreign currency risk, and investment portfolio risk.
- Interest Rate Risk is the risk of financial loss from changes in market interest rates.
- Foreign Exchange Risk is the potential for loss of earnings or capital resulting from fluctuations in currency values. MFIs most often experience this risk when they borrow or mobilize savings in foreign currency and lend in local currency.
- Investment Portfolio Risk refers to longer-term investment decisions rather than short-term liquidity or cash management decisions.

Operational Risk

- Human Resources Risk.
- Information and Technology Risk is the potential that inadequate technology and information systems will result in unexpected losses.
- Fraud Risk is the risk of loss of earnings or capital as a result of intentional deception by an employee or client.
- Regulatory and Legal Compliance Risk is the risk of loss resulting from non-compliance with the country's regulations and laws.

Strategic Risk

- Governance Risk is the risk of having an inadequate structure or body to make effective decisions.

Institutional Risk

- Social Mission
- Commercial Mission
- Dependency
- Strategic
- Reputation

External Risks

- Regulatory
- Competition
- Demographic
- Macroeconomic
- Environmental
- Political

Top 50 Microfinance Institutions

Please follow this link :

http://www.forbes.com/2007/12/20/microfinance-philanthropy-credit-biz-cz_ms_1220microfinance_table.html

M-CRIL INDIA INDICES OF MICROFINANCE 2011

M-CRIL India Indices of Microfinance 2011, is a measure of the performance of the 24 largest MFIs in India. The indices indicate, that the growth of the largest Indian MFIs in 2010-11 has declined to a very low level

CRILEX – the M-CRIL India MFI Growth Index

FINEX – the M-CRIL India Financial Performance Index

FINEX – the M-CRIL India Financial Performance Index is a composite index of the performance of microfinance institutions in India. It uses information on the portfolio at risk

(>30 days) and the return on assets of 24 leading MFIs

(based on financial information self-reported by the MFIs to the MIX)

FINEX has declined to

-466

(March 2003=100 in the Figure 1)

Compared to the 40% increase in 2008-09 and a 10% increase in 2009-10.

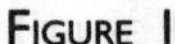

FIGURE 1

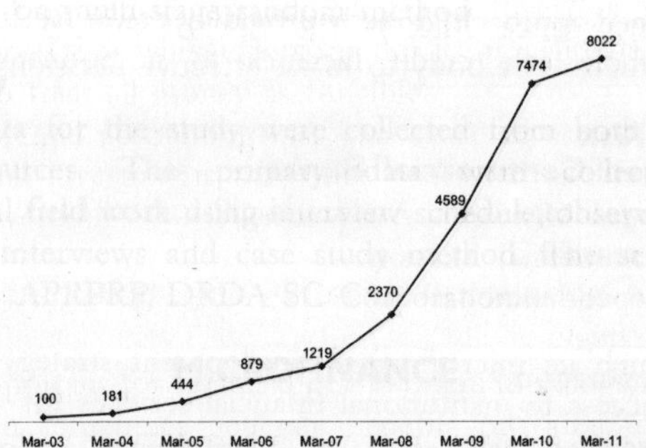

FIGURE 2

Annual Growth Rates

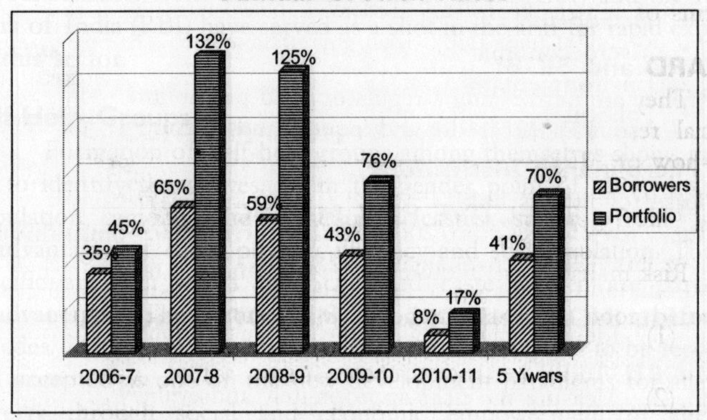

M-Cril24, March 2003=100

By 31 March 2011, CRILEX had reached 8,022 (March 2003=100 in the Figure 2)

Growth in 2010-11 was just 7.5% for borrowers and 7.2% for portfolio, greatly reduced from the 43% and 76% growth respectively in the previous year after adjusting for multiple lending.

Growth has not been even; the four largest MFIs operating in AP recorded negligible growth rates for the year. Other MFIs grew at 10-15%, and a few at 40-50%.

PILLARS OF MICROFINANCE IN INDIA

Niche Market Microfinance in India

Institutes such as Spandana, Share Microfinance Ltd. and SKS Finance have also scaled up their microcredit outreach dramatically in recent years.

Private Banks like ICICI Bank

Expanding its financial services to poor households through a multi-prolonged approach, directly providing credit facilities to SHG, and providing whole sale credit facilities to microfinance NGO's and NBFC's.

State Owned Commercial Banks

The Syndicate bank, Andhra bank, Canara bank, Indian bank has entered this market.

ADB

Through its microfinance development strategy aims to assure permanent access to institutional financial services for the regions poor and their small business.

Private Equity Firms

Started to eye the low profile MFI's as they see huge potential in its terms of returns from this sector.

NABARD and SIDBI

They are performing a regulatory and promotional role providing financial resources as credit and equity and enhancing technological know-how of MFI's.

EFFECTIVE RISK MANAGEMENT

Risk management requires an organization to take four key steps:

(1) Identify the risks facing the institution and assess their severity;
(2) Measure the risks appropriately and evaluate the acceptable limits for that risk;
(3) Monitor the risks on a routine basis, ensuring that the right people receive accurate and relevant information; and
(4) Manage the risks through close oversight and evaluation of performance.

ACCION CAMEL

CAMEL is an acronym for five measurements of a financial institution: Capital adequacy, Asset quality, Management, Earnings, and Liquidity management.

CAMEL was created initially to enable North American bank regulators to measure the financial and managerial soundness of U.S. commercial lending institutions using key ratios, indicators, and institutional policies and procedures.

Based on the results of the adjusted financial statements and interviews with the MFI's management and staff, a rating of one to five is assigned to each of the CAMEL's 21 indicators and weighted accordingly. A definition of each area and the criteria ranges for determining each rating are as follows.

Capital Adequacy

The objective of the capital adequacy analysis is to measure the financial solvency of an MFI by determining whether the risks it has incurred are adequately offset with capital and reserves to absorb potential losses. One indicator is **leverage**, which illustrates the relationship between the risk-weighted assets of the MFI and its equity. Another indicator, **ability to raise equity**, is a qualitative assessment of an MFI's ability to respond to a need to replenish or increase equity at any given time. A third indicator, **adequacy of reserves,** is a quantitative measure of the MFI's loan loss reserve and the degree to which the institution can absorb potential loan losses.

Asset Quality

The analysis of asset quality is divided into three components: portfolio quality, portfolio classification system, and fixed assets. Portfolio quality includes two quantitative indicators: **portfolio at risk**, which measures the portfolio past due over 30 days; and **write-offs/write-off policy**, which measures the MFI's adjusted write-offs based on CAMEL criteria. Portfolio classification system entails reviewing the portfolio's aging schedules and assessing the institution's policies associated with assessing portfolio risk.

Under fixed assets, one indicator is the **productivity of long-term assets**, which evaluates the MFI's policies for investing in fixed assets. The other indicator concerns the institution's **infrastructure**, which is evaluated to determine whether it meets the needs of both staff and clients.

Management

Five qualitative indicators make up this area of analysis: **governance; human resources; processes, controls, and audit; information technology system; and strategic planning and budgeting.**

Governance focuses on how well the institution's board of director's functions, including the diversity of its technical expertise, its independence from management, and its ability to make decisions flexibly and effectively.

Human resources, evaluates whether the department of human resources provides clear guidance and support to operations staff, including recruitment and training of new personnel, incentive systems for personnel, and performance evaluation system. **Processes, controls,**

and audit, focuses on the degree to which the MFI has formalized key processes and the effectiveness with which it controls risk throughout the organization.

Information technology system, assesses whether computerized information systems are operating effectively and efficiently, and are generating reports for management purposes in a timely and accurate manner. This analysis reviews the information technology environment and the extent and quality of the specific information technology controls.

Strategic planning and budgeting, looks at whether the institution undertakes a comprehensive and participatory process for generating short- and long-term financial projections and whether the plan is updated as needed and used in the decision-making process.

Earnings

The ACCION CAMEL chooses three quantitative and one qualitative indicator to measure the profitability of MFIs: adjusted return on equity, operational efficiency, adjusted return on assets, and interest rate policy. **Adjusted return on equity (ROE)** measures the ability of the institution to maintain and increase its net worth through earnings from operations. **Operational efficiency** measures the efficiency of the institution and monitors its progress toward achieving a cost structure that is closer to the level achieved by formal financial institutions. **Adjusted return on assets (ROA)** measures how well the MFI's assets are utilized, or the institution's ability to generate earnings with a given asset base. CAMEL analysts also study the MFI's **interest rate policy** to assess the degree to which management analyzes and adjusts the institution's interest rates on microenterprise loans based on the cost of funds, profitability targets, and macroeconomic environment.

Liquidity Management

The fifth area of the ACCION CAMEL evaluates the MFI's ability to accommodate decreases in funding sources and increases in assets and to pay expenses at a reasonable cost. Indicators in this area are liability structure, availability of funds to meet credit demand, cash flow projection

CONCLUSION

The microfinance industry has experienced dramatic growth during the last two decades, in general, and the last decade, in particular. The next decade will most probably see a continuation of this growth. Such growth is not only sought by many MFIs but also needed in most countries because the unserved and underserved markets continue to remain large. However, pursuit of growth—in terms of breadth, depth, and scope of outreach—does not mean that MFIs can ignore risk management. In contrast, risk management has become more important now than it was 10 years ago, and its importance will continue to grow. Other factors such as the increasing competition in markets and the integration of new technology into the industry further reinforce the importance of microfinance risk management.

References

Books

Beatriz Armendariz Marc Labie, 2008, *"The Handbook of Microfinance"*, by World Scientific Publishing Co. Pvt. Ltd. , ISBN-13-978-981-4295-65-9.

Margurtite, S. Robinson, *"The Microfinance Revolution: Sustainable Finance for the Poor"*, USA, ISBN-08213-4521-9.

Mike Goldberg and Eric Palladini, *"Managing risk and creating value with microfinance"*, by Washington, DC, ISBN -978-0-8213-8228-8.

Jan-Hendrik Boerse, Foreign Exchange and Disaster Risk Management in Microfinance Institutions, ISBN-978-3-640-22258.

Websites

http://pdf.usaid.gov/pdf_docs/PNACE721.pdf

http://www.nabard.org/FileUpload/DataBank/AnnualReports/Nabard_AR_Eng_2011_(Fianl)[1].pdf

http://www.iimahd.ernet.in/~mssriram/microfinance-RT.pdf

http://www.slideshare.net/kabrapiyush/microfinance-introduction-small

http://www2.adb.org/Documents/Papers/Managing-Microfinance-Risks/Managing-Microfinance-Risks.pdf

http://www.gdrc.org/icm/disasters/microfinance_drm.pdf

http://dissertations.ub.rug.nl/FILES/faculties/feb/2011/r.j.galema/07_concl.pdf

http://www.m-cril.com/

http://www.microfinancefocus.com/m-cril-india-indices-microfinance-2011-download

http://www.mixmarket.org/mfi/country/India/news/blank?page=31&PHPSESSID=c955d9068d1e40be8b5f697140163cfc

http://www.ibtimes.com/articles/74817/20101022/m-cril-india-indices-of-microfinance-crilex-growth-index-india-financial-performance.htm

http://www.citigroup.com/citi/microfinance/news.htm

http://articles.economictimes.indiatimes.com/2011-01-13/news/28425980_1_mfis-trident-microfin-kishore-kumar-puli

http://www.humana-india.org/index.php?option=com_content&view=article&id=553&Itemid=248

9

A Conceptual Study of SKS Microfinance in India

DR. MANOJ KUMAR

1. INTRODUCTION

"Microcredit, or microfinance, is banking the unbankables, bringing credit, savings and other essential financial services within the reach of millions of people who are too poor to be served by regular banks, in most cases because they are unable to offer sufficient collateral. In general, banks are for people with money, not for people without." (Gert van Maanen, Microcredit: Sound Business or Development Instrument, Oikocredit, 2004).

A good definition of microfinance as provided by Robinson is, 'Microfinance refers to small-scale financial services for both credits and deposits—that are provided to people who farm or fish or herd; operate small or micro enterprises where goods are produced, recycled, repaired, or traded; provide services; work for wages or commissions; gain income from renting out small amounts of land, vehicles, draft animals, or machinery and tools; and to other individuals and local groups in developing countries, in both rural and urban areas'.

2. OVERVIEW OF SKS

SKS began operations in the Telangana region of Andhra

Pradesh, part of the drought-prone, semi-arid Deccan Plateau, one of the poorest parts of India. Over the last 10 years, SKS has continued to work in regions which suffer from high rates of hunger and malnutrition. These regions have significant numbers of poor who are landless laborers or marginal farmers drawing a livelihood from subsistence agriculture. The income (most of them earn less than $1 a day) is not enough to provide their families with basic necessities like food, healthcare and education. SKS provides them loans to enable them involve in income generating activities like livestock, agriculture, trade, production and services.

Launched in 1998, SKS Microfinance is one of the fastest growing microfinance organizations in the world, having provided over US $ 1.2 Billion (Rs. 6,212 crore) and has maintained loans outstanding of US$ 427 Million (Rs. 2,216 crore) in loans to 39,06,007 women members in poor regions of India. Borrowers take loans for a range of income-generating activities, including livestock, agriculture, trade (such as vegetable vending), production (from basket weaving to pottery) and new age businesses (Beauty Parlor to photography). SKS also offers interest-free loans for emergencies as well as life insurance to its members. Its NGO wing SKS foundation runs the Ultra Poor Program.

SKS is headquartered in Hyderabad and currently has microfinance branches in 18 states across India. SKS aims to reach members 15,000,000 by 2012. In the last year alone, SKS Microfinance has achieved nearly 170% growth, with 99% on-time repayment rate. It is one of the top most microfinance institution of India. SKS currently only targets women both because they are the most marginalized and because they tend to use resources more productively than men. Social science research has shown that women tend to undertake small, manageable activities rather than risky ventures and they invest the majority of their income into the household and for their children. Currently SKS operates with 1,354 branches in 18 states across India.

3. RATE OF INTEREST

According to Vikram Akula 28% is actually what loan sharks typically seem to charge and so it certainly seems high but what in fact is the situation is that commercial banks simply don't move in this space. They are not able to have the systems to reach out to the poor in villages so it is not that the poor get a lower interest rate from the commercial banks in fact they have no alternative but to turn to moneylenders who charge exploitive rates of interest SKS offers a range of working capital and consumption loans. SKS working capital products provide financing for various income generating incomes in the areas of trade, service, agriculture and production. Loans are used for everything from buying buffalo (to selling milk) to opening kirana shops. These loans have a flat rate of 12.5 per cent and a total effective rate of 28 per cent. SKS consumption loan or emergency loan is an interest-free loan. This loan serves to provide cushioning during difficult times.

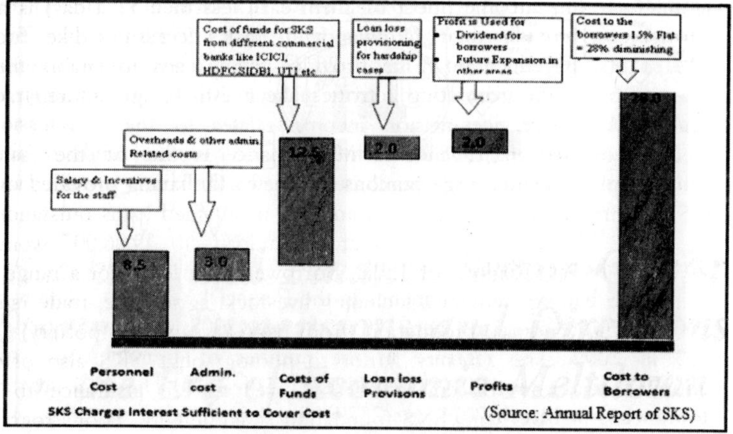

SKS Charges Interest Sufficient to Cover Cost (Source: Annual Report of SKS)

4. EVALUATION OF SKS

The poor have no access to financial services that they need. This financial exclusion leads to the creation of a society where the poor lack opportunity. They pay a premium for products and services due to this. SKS aims to bridge this gap and bring the complete range of financial services to the doorsteps of its members. It also aims at adding value by using its network to distribute quality products and services that its members need.

4.1 Financial Performance

4.1.1 Income From Operations

Income from operations increased by 32.9% to Rs. 1,160.2 crore in fiscal 2011 from Rs. 872.9 crore in fiscal 2010. This growth is primarily due to an increase in average gross loan portfolio by 38.5% from Rs. 3,388.6 crore in fiscal 2010 to Rs. 4,694.4 crore in fiscal 2011. The opening and closing gross loan portfolio for the fiscal 2011 was Rs. 4,320.7 crore (March 2010) and Rs. 4,110.7 crore (March 2011) respectively.

4.1.2 Other Income

Other income increased by 27.8% to Rs. 109.3 crore in fiscal 2011 from Rs. 85.6 crore in fiscal 2010. The rise in other income is primarily due to an increase in income from group insurance administrative charges by Rs. 38.5 crore. There is a decrease in income from insurance commission by Rs. 8.7 crore, as SKS stopped the pilot project of distribution of new life insurance policies from May 2010. Interest income from fixed deposits decreased by Rs. 11.0 crore in fiscal 2011 due to a decrease in cash and bank balances from Rs. 973.5 crore in fiscal 2010 to Rs. 557.9 crore in fiscal 2011. Other commission income increased by 19.7% from Rs. 3.2 crore in fiscal 2010 to Rs. 3.9 crore in fiscal 2011. Other commission income relates to the commission received from strategic alliance partners on sale of other products such as mobile phones and on the purchases made by the kirana stores owned by SKS borrowers.

4.2 Branches of SKS

SKS had only 276 branches in the Financial Year 2007. The total branches of the company were 770 in the year 2008, which increased to 1353 in 2009. The increase in the number of branches was still continuing in the year 2010 when it reached to 2029. The total number of branches in March 2011 was 2379. The compounded annual growth rate of the company branches comes to around 71%.

Total Number of Branches of SKS

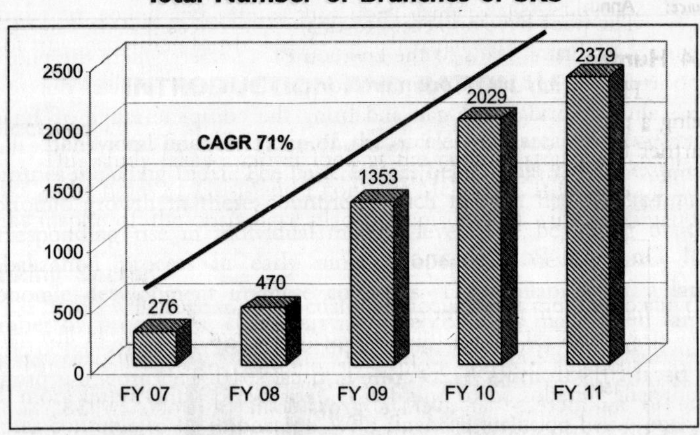

Source: Annual Report of SKS.

4.3 Coverage Area of SKS

The districts covered by the SKS have been constantly increasing day-by-day. In the Financial Year 2007 the company has got its existence in only 103 districts. The number of districts has increased to 219 in the year 2008. This rapid increase in the expansion of the business area was further continued and has reached to 378 districts in the financial year 2011. The compounded annual growth rate was 38% regarding the increase in the number of districts.

Total Number of Branches of SKS

Source: Annual Report of SKS.

4.4 Human Resources Management

Human Resources (HR) has made a successful journey from being a prompt basic service provider to becoming a Business/Strategic Partner for the organization. Last year was a remarkable period for the

Increase in Employees of SKS

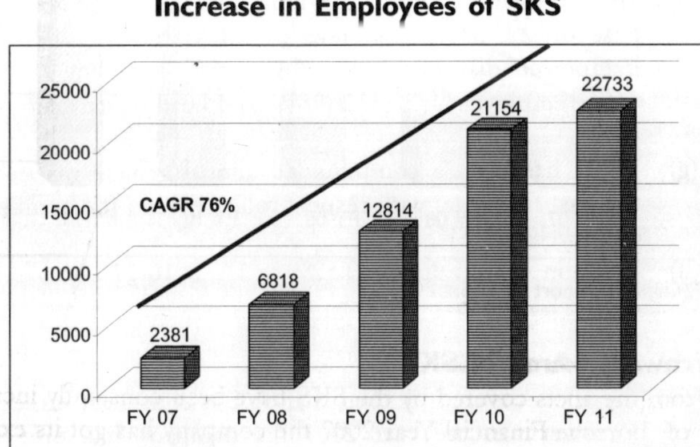

Source: Annual Report of SKS.

SKS, and this has given an opportunity to HR to help employees understand changes in the internal and external environment as well as to support business goals by designing various interventions and employee engagement initiatives—

(a) HR has introduced various mechanisms for building and strengthening an inclusive culture at SKS, like creating a platform to meet the field staff across 19 states, being accessible to each and every employee through a toll free number for employees facilitating skip-level meetings and mobile-enabled services.

(b) Around 21.96% of employees have been covered under the Employee Stock Option Plans (ESOP) and the Employee Share Purchase Scheme (ESPS) with a primary focus on retention, productivity and co-creation of wealth as well as a sense of ownership in the Company.

(c) The Company has also strengthened the behavioral and managerial skills of employees to build an internal talent pipeline. The Learning and Development team has carried out about 17,630 hours of training across India.

(d) SKS has a dedicated team of 250 trainers who have successfully delivered 3,65,042 hours of technical training for field force in nine major Indian languages. The training covers areas like processes, products and policies with a robust testing mechanism measuring the effectiveness of programs.

(e) Initiated Supervisory Skills Training Program for Branch Managers.

(f) HR has been promptly providing services to the employee base of 22,733 across India as on March 31, 2011. The manpower distribution is: field staff including regional office employees—22,332 (98%) and head office staff—401 (2%).

(g) There has been a compounded annual growth of 76% in the past five years with respect to increase in the number of employees of SKS.

(h) Attrition moved up to 29.52% in FY 2010-11 compared to 25.7% last year.

4.5 Borrowers from SKS

From the above figure it is clear that SKS is constantly increasing its base of borrowers. In the year 2007 the company had only 6.04 million borrowers. In the year 2008 there were only 18.79 million borrowers of the company. It has increased to 39.53 million in 2009 which is more than double the borrowers that the company had in 2008. This growth further continued in the year 2010 when borrowers reached to 67.80 million. At the end of March 2011, SKS had 73.07 million borrowers. Thus it is very much clear that the company is constantly increasing its borrower's base. There is a recorded growth of more than 400% members in the last 4 years. The company has the compounded annual growth rate of 87% for the past 5 years. The company provided loans to the public for the various activities like Agriculture (6%), Livestock (27%), Production (7%), Trade (32%), Services (27%). (The details of the inter-head activities can be seen from the Annexure 3)

Total Number of Borrowers (in Million)

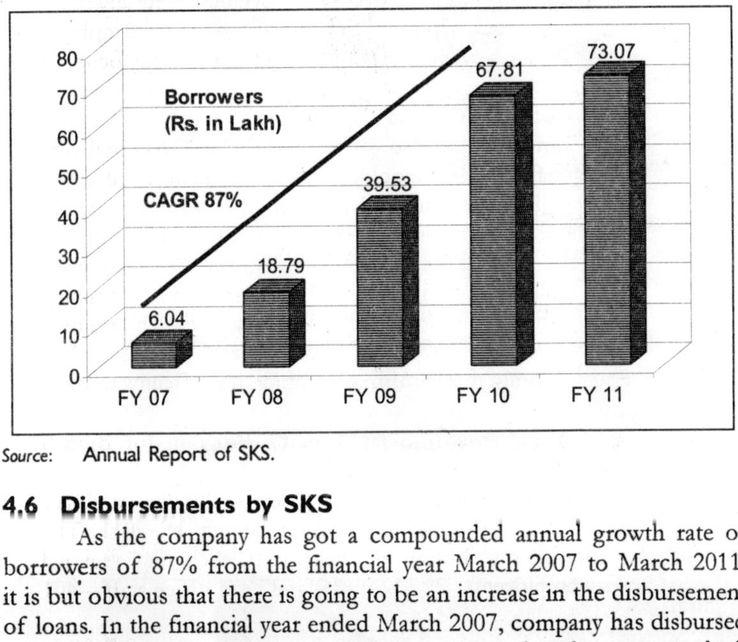

Source: Annual Report of SKS.

4.6 Disbursements by SKS

As the company has got a compounded annual growth rate of borrowers of 87% from the financial year March 2007 to March 2011, it is but obvious that there is going to be an increase in the disbursement of loans. In the financial year ended March 2007, company has disbursed loans of Rs. 452 crore to 6.04 million borrowers that the company had. The amount of loan disbursed to the borrowers increased to Rs. 1680 crore at the end of the financial year 2008. There was an overall increase of 3.71 times as compared to the previous financial year. The increase in loan further continued in the year 2009 when it reached to Rs. 4485 crore. The disbursement of loan was increased to Rs. 7618 crore and Rs. 7831 crore in the financial year ended March 2010 and 2011. The company has recorded a compounded annual growth rate of 104% for the financial year ended March 2007 to March 2011.

Amount Disbursed (INR in Crores)

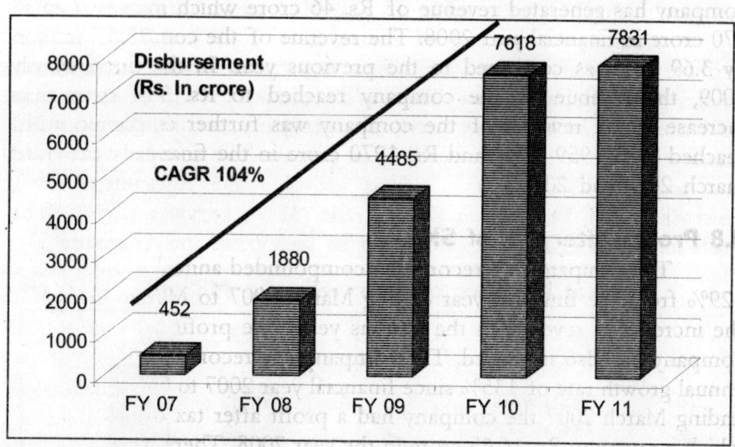

Source: Annual Report of SKS.

4.7 Revenue of SKS

As the number of borrowers of the company is increasing at a compounded annual growth rate of 87% and the amount of loans disbursed to these borrowers has increased at a compounded annual growth rate of 104%, it is but obvious that there should be an increase in the revenue of the company. The revenue of the company has also

Total Revenue (INR in Crores)

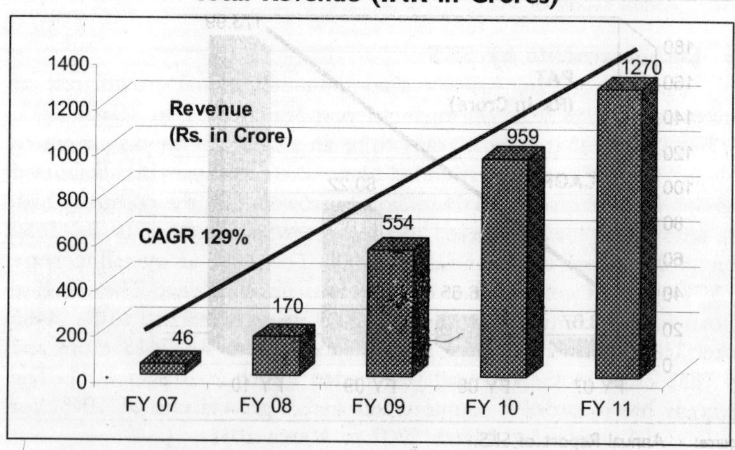

Source: Annual Report of SKS.

increased at an compounded annual growth rate of 129% for the financial year ended March 2007 to March 2011. In the year 2007 company has generated revenue of Rs. 46 crore which increased to Rs. 170 crore in financial year 2008. The revenue of the company increased by 3.69 times as compared to the previous year. In the financial year 2009, the revenue of the company reached to Rs. 554 crore. This increase in the revenue of the company was further continued and it reached to Rs. 959 crore and Rs. 1270 crore in the financial year ended march 2010 and 2011.

4.8 Profits After Tax of SKS

The company had recorded a compounded annual growth rate of 129% from the financial year ending March 2007 to March 2011. With the increase in revenue in the various years, the profit after tax of the company has also increased. The company has recorded a compounded annual growth rate of 135% since financial year 2007 to 2011. In the year ending March 2007 the company had a profit after tax of Rs. 3.6 crore which increase to Rs. 16.65 crore in the year 2008. There was an increase of 4.53 times in the profit after tax of the company. The increase in the profit after tax was continued and it reached to Rs. 80.22 crore in the financial year 2009. In the financial year ending March 2010 the profit after tax of the company increased to Rs. 173.95 crore. The profit of the company declined in the financial year 2011 and it fell to Rs. 111.63 crore. The fall in the profit of the company was due to the provisions and write offs which amounted to Rs. 236.2 crore which was 18.6% of the revenue earned by the company in financial year 2011.

PAT (INR in Crores)

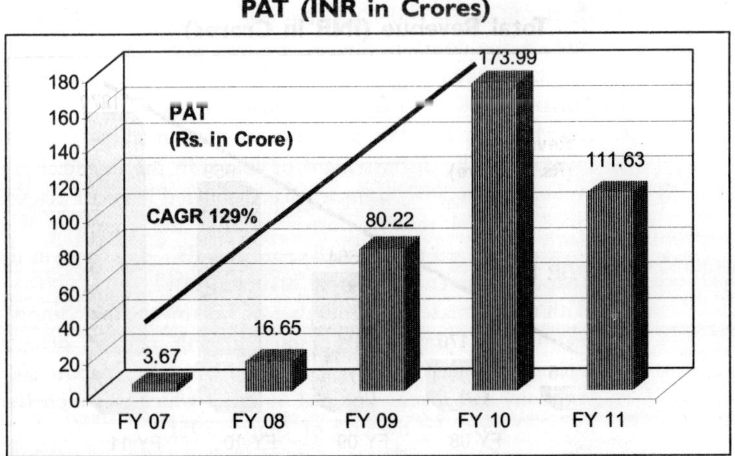

Source: Annual Report of SKS.

5. CONCLUSION

SKS maintained its leadership position in the industry with total disbursements of Rs. 7,831 crore and a borrower base of 73.1 lakh (7.3 million) in fiscal 2011. The company also became the only Indian MFI to make a public offer, thereby tapping capital market resources to meet credit needs of rural households. As a responsible leader, it has always followed ethical practices and processes in dealing with borrowers:

(a) SKS had only 276 branches in the Financial Year 2007 which increased to 2379 at the end of the financial year ending March 2011. The compounded annual growth rate of the company comes to around 71%.

(b) The districts covered by the SKS have been constantly increasing day by day. In the Financial Year 2007 the company has got its existence in only 103 districts which had increased to 378 by the end of the financial year ending March 2011. The compounded annual growth rate was 38% regarding the increase in the number of districts.

(c) The company had only 2,381 employees in the year 2007. This number was increased to 22,733 by the end of the financial year ending March 2011. The compounded annual growth rate of the increase in the company employees was 76% during the last five years.

(d) The borrowers of the company are constantly increasing. The company had got only 1.8 million borrowers in the year 2008, which increased to 7.3 million borrowers by the end of the financial year 2011. The compounded annual growth rate of the company during the past five years was 87%.

(e) The company has got a compounded annual growth rate of borrowers of 87% from the financial year March 2007 to March 2011, it is but obvious that there is going to be an increase in the disbursement of loans. In the financial year ended March 2007, company has disbursed loans of Rs. 452 crore to 6.04 million borrowers that the company had, which increased to Rs. 7618 crore and Rs. 7831 crore in the financial year ended March 2010 and 2011.

(f) With the increase in the number of borrowers, the company recorded a compounded annual growth rate of revenue during the past five years was 129%. In March 2007 company had revenue of just 46 crore which was increased to 1270 crore by the end of March 2011.

(g) The profit of the company has continuously been increasing. In the financial year ended March 2007 company had a profit after tax of Rs. 3.67 crore. The profit of the company increased to a level of Rs. 111.63 crore by the end of the financial year ending March 2011. The company recorded compounded annual growth in the profit after tax of 129% during the last five years.

(h) SKS has identified the barriers to scaling microfinance, what it calls the 3 Cs of Capital, Capacity and Costs. It has taken an innovative approach to overcome these barriers. These three principles, using a profit-oriented model, drawing on best practices from the business world for scaling and using technology have helped us create a new generation of microfinance institution and enabled us to reach numbers that otherwise the microfinance sector has not seen before.

6. BARRIERS IN THE GROWTH OF SKS

SKS Microfinance was in the news recently and this concerned cash embezzlements and frauds for the financial year 2011. As Microfinance Focus notes, "According to auditors, SKS Microfinance recorded 408 cases of cash embezzlements and frauds in the financial year 2011. The company's annual report shows 156 cases of cash embezzlements by the employees aggregating Rs. 1,60,18,106 during 2011. There were 205 cases of loans given out to non-existent borrowers on the basis of fictitious documentation created by the employees of the company aggregating Rs. 4,51,77,531. Further, 47 cases of loans taken by borrowers under fake identity aggregating Rs. 1,37,86,130 were reported during the year. The Company is pursuing the borrowers to repay the money. The outstanding loan balance (net of recovery) aggregating Rs. 63,86,267 has been written-off.

6.1 Loan Disbursement Related Frauds

The loan disbursement frauds mainly included: (a) Loan officer issues loans to "ghost" or non-existent clients. (b) Loan officer issues 2nd or 3rd loan to delinquent clients to facilitate repayment (top-up or greening of loans and this is very evident from cases of clients with multiple loans). (c) Loan officer provides bulk money to agents for onward disbursement and has no serious means to check their actual disbursement to clients. In many cases, these loans are used for non-micro-finance activities. (d) Staff/cashier/accountant makes loans to themselves and show fictitious names or clients with false identities. (e) Loan officer charges clients an unofficial "fee" (BAKSHISH) from clients to enable them to access a loan from an MFI. (e) Loan officer, staff, accountant, cashier issue larger loans to clients and use some portion of the loan for their own consumption. They however do not repay and expect the client to repay and this is an important reason for delinquency. (f) Several other aspects.

6.2 Loan Repayment Related Frauds

This kind of fraud mainly included: (a) Loan officer collects payment, issues receipt, but does not deposit the money repaid (by the client) with the MFI. This could happen with client prepayments or regular payments. (b) Agents collect loan payments and do not deposit them in a timely manner with the concerned MFI. Agents who have not lent money to clients but rather used loan amounts from MFI, do not repay the MFI at all. (c) Staff/loan officer charges unofficial delinquency fees to manage delinquency. (d) Loan officer/others collect payments on loans that have been officially written off and keep it themselves. (e) Several other aspects.

6.3 Other Kinds of Frauds

The other kinds of frauds include: (a) Insurance payments do not reach the client nominees who in the course of time forget to ask for them. (b) Insurance premiums are not deposited at the branch. (c) Higher than required insurance payments are collected in the guise of administrative charges (please do recall that IRDA recently initiated an enquiry against a large Indian MFI).

7. SUGGESTIONS

- Microfinance is rapidly expanding across India but mobile banking would speed and lengthen its reach to the country's most remote corners. The cumbersome task of manually handling small loans would become safer and far more efficient. Whatever the concern successful mobile banking systems around the world demonstrate that a wide range of issues can be addressed. Vodafone's M-PESA service in Kenya has grown to 6.5 million customers in the two years since its launch. It has been invaluable in expanding microfinance in a country where law and order problems would hinder and endanger loan officers in the field. In the Philippines, a service called GCASH has been thriving since 2004.
- A consumer grievance redressal process should be created as part of a larger structure for consumer protection, as suggested by the Committee for Financial Sector Reforms (myriad agencies for grievances will increase confusion and costs).

- Regulation that sets strict interest rate ceilings should be avoided, regulation should reward MFIs that charge reasonable interest rates as well as those that introduce innovative products that provide flexibility in repayment. For instance, built-in insurance that protects the borrower during times of distress.
- The establishment of a well-functioning credit bureau to which all MFIs are required to report their entire portfolio of lending is key to preventing over-indebtedness. The introduction of Unique IDs greatly facilitates the establishment of such a bureau that would benefit the industry as a whole.
- MFIs recently created a Microfinance Institutions Network (MFIN) that adopted a code of conduct that focuses on fair practices with borrowers. The industry should accelerate MFIN implementation as well as the credit bureau. The RBI should examine, approve and monitor the implementation of this code of conduct, which could form the basis of future regulation.
- SKS is well capitalized and is in a strong position to benefit from the consolidation in the sector. The company should follow the following strategy:
    1. **Consolidation:** It should consolidate its leadership position and focus on meeting the various needs of its existing borrowers rather than acquiring new ones.
    2. **Diversification:** The company should scale earlier pilots on fee-based services and secured lending, gradually converting them into business verticals.
    3. **Resolve the Andhra Pradesh situation:** It is actively engaged with the regulators, the State Government and borrowers to rebuild the sector in the State. The companys' special leave petition challenging the Andhra Pradesh MFI Act has been admitted by the Honourable Supreme Court of India.

When it works well microfinance can be a win-win situation, as the poor can borrow money at rates that may look high but are much lower than those offered by moneylenders and banks can make a sustainable business in lending to the poor. All this rests as much on a social contract as on a legal contract. MFIs need to be more diligent in their lending and screen borrowers better if too many borrowers cannot repay their loans, the social obligation will start to fall apart. But politicians also need to be wary in taking aim at the occasional overstep, they may find themselves inadvertently destroying the whole business, at great cost both to the poor and the financial institutions that have stepped in to work with them. If we are not careful we may end up in the pre-microfinance world. That would be a great disservice to the poor and their hope of climbing out of poverty.

References

A.H. Dewan, Alamgir, 1999, Microfinancial Services in Bangladesh, Review of Innovations and Trends, Dhaka, CDF, Dhaka,

An IPO is a Progression, May 2010, Outlook Business, p. 26.

Capitalism *vs.* Altruism: SKS Rekindles the Microfinance Debate Published: October 07, 2010 in India Knowledge@Wharton

Existing Legal and Regulatory Framework for the Microfinance Institutions in India: Challenges and Implications, Sa-Dhan Microfinance Resource Centre, Edition: 2006.

Sinha, Frances (2005), Access, Use and Contribution of Microfinance in India: Findings from a National Study.

http://www.thehindubusinessline.com/2006/11/21/stories/2006112100390900.htm

http://economictimes.indiatimes.com/articleshow/1648287.cms

http://www.microfinancegateway.org/content/article/detail/49567 - 51k

http://www.thehindubusinessline.in/2010/04/30/stories/2010043050581100.htm

http://www.thehindubusinessline.in/2011/01/15/stories/2011011550150800.htm

http://www.indianexpress.com/news/help-microfinance-dont-kill-it/716105/0

http://www.hindustantimes.com/StoryPage/Print.aspx?Id=cc3fd5af-3718-4f70-8ca4-c99e6d399af3

Sriram, M.S. and Upadhyayula, Rajesh, S., 2002, The Transformation of the Microfinance Sector in India: Experiences, Options and Future.

Reserve Bank of India, Circular RPCD NO.PL.BC. 62/04.09.01/99-2000, Mumbai, February 2000.

SKS Annual Report, 2010-11, 2009-10, 2008-09.

Microfinance and Women Empowerment—Small Amounts Making Big Difference

Nandita Majumdar

"When the women are empowered, the society with stability gets assured".

—*Dr. Abdul Kalam.*

INTRODUCTION

Women workers throughout the world contribute to the economic growth and sustainable livelihoods of their families and communities on par with men. Yet they face many socio-cultural attitude, legal barriers, lack of education and personal difficulties. They are rarely financially independent and often they are more vulnerable members of society. Inspite of a lot of efforts from the government as well as the non-government organization, yet they have no access to credit and other financial services. Therefore, the empowerment of women attracted many sectors of the society.

Microfinance too often target women. The goal is to engender the process of development and eradicate the differences of men and women in economic conditions. Many development agencies realize that women's empowerment is the key to long-term poverty alleviation. It is a tool used to increase the self-reliance of poor people, especially poor women. Women if given chance to develop proved to be better entrepreneurs when compared to men.

Unlike urban areas, the rural areas are more dependable on one another for their day to day needs. To distribute the work, it is seen that they form different groups to enhance their abilities. One such example is the formation of 'chit fund groups' by the homemakers of the rural areas. They all pooled their money in small amounts and on rotation gathered a lump sum of amount for their needs.

The concept of microfinance is similar to this for them. It provided loans, helped them to save for future and other such activities. Microfinance programmes for women are more and more promoted not only as a strategy for poverty alleviation, but also for the empowerment of women (Mayoux, 1996). These programmes have an impact not only on the target group but also on the society in which they live in. Women are seen as more creditworthy than men and hence the bulk of microfinance is directed towards them. It has been reported that corporate giants such as Hindustan Levers Ltd., use women from SHGs to help sell their brands of products like shampoos, oils and soaps.

The microfinance movement gathered its momentum, with women at the grassroots organising themselves into self-help groups (SHGs). In 1991-92, the National Bank for Agriculture and Rural Development (NABARD) decided on a coordinated programme for the promotion of linkages between banks and SHGs to mobilise savings in rural areas and to deliver credit to the rural poor.

OBJECTIVES

The study is humble effort to understand the role of women in present economy. It is to discuss the role of microfinance in women empowerment. It is further focused to know the changes bought by microfinance in women's life and society

LITERATURE REVIEW

Every aspect of society talks about empowerment, the term tough used very often has its own meaning in every different context. The term has been used more often to advocate for certain types of policies and intervention strategies than to analyze them, as demonstrated by a number of documents from the United Nations (UNDAW, 2001; UNICEF, 1999), the Association for Women in Development (Everett, 1991), Feminist activist writings often promote empowerment of individuals and organizations of women but vary in the extent to which they conceptualize or discuss how to identify it.

Empowerment implies expansion of assets and capabilities of people to influence control and hold accountable institution that affects their lives (World Bank Resource Book). Empowerment is the process of enabling or authorizing an individual to think, behave, take action and control work in an autonomous way. It is the state of feelings of self-empowered to take control of one's own destiny. It includes both controls over resources (Physical, Human, Intellectual and Financial) and over ideology (Belief, values and attitudes) (Batliwala, 1994).

Opinions on the impact of microfinance have been divided between those who see it as a "magic bullet" for women's empowerment and others who are dismissive of its abilities as a cure-all panacea for development. It becomes apparent that while access to financial services can and does make vital contributions to the economic productivity and social well-being of poor women and their households, it does not "automatically" empower women, just as with other interventions, such as education, political quotas, etc. that seek to bring about a radical structural transformation that true empowerment entails. (Naila Kabeer)

METHODOLOGY

The paper is a descriptive research paper. The study is based on the resources gathered from secondary data source. The source provided different concepts on microfinance, role of microfinance in women's life, women empowerment through microfinance, SHGs impact on women empowerment, etc. in journals, books, magazines, research work.

WOMEN ROLE IN ECONOMY

Women play a major role in Indian society. She is represented in the forms of Shakti, Lakshmi, Sàraswathi and Kali. The status of women changed 360 degrees in the past few millenniums. From a largely unknown status in ancient times through the low points of the medieval period, to the promotion of equal rights by many reformers, the history of women in India has been unbelievably changed

Government and non-government organizations both have their own contribution in development of women. The Constitution of India guarantees to all Indian women equality (Article 14), no discrimination by the State (Article 15(1)), equality of opportunity (Article 16), equal pay for equal work (Article 39(d)). In addition, it allows special provisions to be made by the State in favour of women and children (Article 15(3)), renounces practices derogatory to the dignity of women (Article 51(A)(e)), and also allows for provisions to be made by the State for securing just and humane conditions of work and for maternity relief (Article 42).

Almost 50% of our population today comprises women while

42% is under the age of 18. It shows the major power and human resource for our country is young to create new wonders. It is observed that Women are significant contributors to the growing economy. For growth to be truly inclusive, we have to ensure their protection, well-being, development, empowerment and participation.

India has committed to meeting the MDGs and is a signatory to many international conventions, including Convention for Elimination of all forms of Discrimination against women. The Government of India declared year 2001 as the year of women's empowerment, with the objective of creating a new century and a nation where women are equal partners with men. A lot of women oriented programmes were introduced, such as Swashakti and Stree Shakti for women's empowerment; Swayam Sidha to benefit 100,000 women through micro-credit programmes and so on. Even the 11th Five Year Plan is very specific about contributing 33% of direct and indirect beneficiaries of all government schemes to women and girl children.

Inspite of all the effort, the sad story is that, they are considered as just the extension of household and her income is supposed to be the second source or supporting source of income to the family.

WHY TARGET WOMEN?

The next important question arise often is Why Target Women? The answer is the probable cause of gender specific barriers faced by women to access education, health, employment and so on.

Research done by UNDP, UNIFEM, and the World Bank, and others, indicates that gender inequalities in developing societies inhibit economic growth and development. It is seen that the society which discriminate on the basis of gender pay the cost of greater poverty, slower economic growth, weaker governance, and a lower living standard of their people. The UNDP also found a very strong correlation between its gender empowerment measure and gender-related development indices and its Human Development Index. Overall, evidence is mounting that improved gender equality is a critical component of any development strategy.

Probably, the other reason is women make up the majority of the low paid, unorganized informal sector of most economies. These statistics are used to justify giving priority to increasing women's access to financial services on the grounds that women are relatively more disadvantaged than men. Even if they earn, Women have shown to spend more of their income on their households; therefore, when women are helped to increase their incomes, the welfare of the whole family is improved. In its report on its survey findings the Special Unit on Microfinance of the UNCDF explains, "Women's success benefits more than one person. Several institutions confirmed the well-documented fact that women are more likely than men to spend their profits on household and family needs. Assisting women therefore generates a multiplier effect that enlarges the impact of the institutions' activities."

Microfinance often targets women, in some cases exclusively. Female clients represent eighty-five percent of the poorest microfinance clients. Therefore, targeting women borrowers makes sense from a public policy view point. The focus on female clients is substantial, as women clients register higher repayment rates. They also contribute larger portions of their income to household consumption than their male counterparts. There is thus a strong business and public policy case for targeting female borrowers.

WHAT IS WOMEN EMPOWERMENT?

Poverty is just not the economic condition, but is much more than that. It means scarcity, non-fulfilment of wants, rights denied, opportunities curtailed, voices silenced, and so on. According to United Nations Millennium Campaign the world poverty can be halved by the year 2015. It is observed that women earn only 10 percent of the world's income and own less than 1 percent of the world's property. Thus, empowering women would be a big challenge faced by the society.

Empowerment is defined as the processes by which women take control and ownership of their lives through expansion of their choices. Thus, it is the process of acquiring the ability to make strategic life choices in a context where this ability has previously been denied. The core elements of empowerment have been defined as agency (the ability to define one's goals and act upon them), awareness of gendered power structures, self-esteem and self-confidence (Kabeer, 2001)

Empowerment is the state of feelings of self-empowered to take control of one's own destiny. It includes both controls over resources (Physical, Human, Intellectual and Financial) and over ideology (Belief, values and attitudes) (Batliwala, 1994).

Empowerment can take place at a hierarchy of different levels—individual, household, community and societal—and is facilitated by providing encouraging factors (e.g., exposure to new activities, which can build capacities) and removing inhibiting factors (e.g., lack of resources and skills).

Need of Empowerment of women changes from society to society. The most important aspects common to all societies are the focus on socio-cultural aspects, political and legal mobilization and economic stabilization of women.

Microfinance acts as a catalyst and works very carefully on the glass ceiling of women's role in economy building of the family. Microfinance work with the help of self-help groups for better work structure. Special funds for women are set aside with the terms "Women's component" to ensure flow of adequate resources for the same. To name a few are Swarnajayanti Grameen Swarazgar Yojona (SGSY), Indira Awas Yojona (IAJ), National Social Assistance Programme (NSAP), Integrated Rural Development Programme (IRDP), the (erstwhile) Development of Women and Children in Rural Areas (DWCRA), the Jawahar Rozgar Yojana (JRY), etc

ROLE OF MICROFINANCE IN WOMEN EMPOWERMENT

The term microfinance has no statutory definition. It is a concept of recent origin mostly dealing with issues related to poverty, alleviation, financial support, gender development, etc.

The taskforce on supportive policy and regulatory framework for microfinance has defined microfinance as "provision of thrift, credit and other financial services and products of very small amounts to the poor in rural, semi-urban or urban areas for enabling them to raise their income levels and improve living standards. In general, the term 'micro' means 'small'. But it is not clearly explained yet how 'small' it is to be.

Microfinance is a magic wand to the poor especially to poor women in the rural areas. To the one who don't know what is banking and its activities, microfinance is a boon in disguise. Microfinance approach is a simple process in working in groups to create capital for their investments, savings for future, credit for needy, etc.

Microfinance in simple terms is the provision of thrift, credit and other financial services and products in very small amounts to the poor for enabling them to raise their income levels and improve living standards. It is the provision of very small loans that are rapid within short periods and is essentially used by low-income individuals and households. Microfinance is enabling, empowering, and bottom up tool to poverty alleviation that has provided considerable economic and non-economic externalities to low income households in developing countries.

The microfinance movement in India was formally launched by the National Bank for Agriculture and Rural Development (NABARD) in 1992. The microfinance scene in India is dominated by SHG-Bank linkage. The primary aim of the SHG-Bank linkage programme is to integrate informal savings and credit groups with mainstream banking system by providing credit facility to groups to enhance their fund base. In this direction, the financial services of banks started routing through SHGs. Thus, a link was established between informal groups (SHGs) and formal financial institutions (banks) for catering the financial needs of the poor. This network helped the banking sector to extend their outreach to the poorest of the poor. NABARD played a crucial role in establishing an effective and strong SHG-Bank linkage programme. The linkage programme focuses on developing credit delivery services for the poor; building a mutual trust and confidence between bankers and the poor; encouraging banking activity both on thrift as well as credit and sustaining a simple and formal mechanism of banking with the poor. Reserve Bank of India provided policy support to SHG-Bank linkage that allowed banks to open savings accounts, relax interest rates, margin security, etc. necessary for SHGs. SHG-Bank linkage programme became the largest and fastest growing finance programme in the world.

SHG is a small autonomous, non political group of people living in the vicinity/neighborhood and sharing common concerns, who come together voluntarily to work jointly for their personal, social and economic development. SHG is a group of 10-20 members who voluntarily associate themselves for common concerns, mainly to eradicate poverty. All the members agree for common savings, generate a common fund and utilize the same for their credit needs through a management.

The objectives of these groups are:

- To provide a cost effective credit delivery system,
- To provide a forum for collective learning,
- To provide genuine democratic culture,
- To provide opportunities to imbibe norms of behavior based on mutual respect,
- To provide a firm and stable base for dialogue,
- To broaden the pattern of asset provision, and
- To foster entrepreneurial culture.

Too much is talked about women empowerment. This discussion is a continuous process, going on from the ancient time through medieval times and still in present. The real momentum of women empowerment started getting its grip from 1970 in many countries.

The problem of women's access to credit was given particular emphasis at the first international women's conference in Mexico in 1975. It focused on the emerging awareness of women's productive role both for national economy and for women's rights, leading to set-up women's world banking network and credit provisions.

From mid-1980s the awareness attained its peak, not only the economist, but even the common people felt the urge of women empowerment. There started pooling of resources by donors, government organizations and non-government organizations, etc.

The 90s saw the rapid development and expansion of microfinance institutions. These organizations lend small amounts to the poor people. To their wonder women were the most honest repayers of loans. This finally led to the increase of emphasis on targeting women

Microfinance has recently been seen a key strategy in meeting not only millennium goal on gender equality, but also poverty reduction, health and others

SMALL AMOUNT MAKING BIG DIFFERENCE

It has been well documented that an increase in women resources or better approach for credit facilities results in increased well-being of the family especially children. (Mayoux, 1997; Kabeer, 2001)

As known microfinance scene in India is dominated by SHG-Bank linkage, the SHG works on very simple principles which provide small amounts making big differences

The SHG works with a set of women forming into groups; these small groups of 10-12 members (depending on the group the number of members vary) revolve the funds so as to multiple the savings along with the external funds. These funds are then rotated among themselves. They in furtherance create income generating activities such as agriculture, poultry, candle making, basket weaving, embroidery, selling vegetables and fruits, pickle and papad making, bee keeping, knitting, manufacturing wood and cane products, and so on. To revolve the fund and attain success the group formation is to be lasting for atleast 6 months.

Self-help groups by which microfinance is provided in small amounts is proved to make a big difference. It is evident through the development of the women and society in many areas. The impact on empowerment was measured on various parameters of self-confidence and are also evident from the following

Economic Empowerment

Economic empowerment results in women's ability to influence or make decisions increase self-confidence, better status and role in household, etc. Microfinance is necessary to overcome exploitation, create confidence for economic self-reliance of the rural poor, particularly among rural women who are mostly invisible in the social structure.

Podupulakshmi phase—a massive thrift movement by 2 lakh women formed into 7000 groups of 20-30 in each have saved over Rs. 8 crores in four years. Today a wide variety of women-centered activities are carried out by these podupulakshmi groups. This is a best example of microfinance impact on women and their effort to save money in small amounts. Poor women became actors for change, able to analyze their own lives, make their own decisions and take their own actions. Women gained ability to act by building awareness, skills, knowledge, confidence and experience.

Political Empowerment

Microfinance not only has developed women's internal confidence by giving financial independence, it also has ensured women the society a better place to live in. Women leaders supported to contribute effectively in local decision-making and to demand quality public services. Women in rural areas are now contesting for local body elections. Bharathi, is one such aspiring leader, a member of SHG and wife of a farmer Vijayarangam of Sedarapet village, aims to renovating the three temples in her village, getting a hospital to take care of emergency cases, widening roads, constructing open drains on roadsides, etc if she is elected as a ward member in the local body election held in Pondicherry.

Social Empowerment

Microfinance initiatives showed the potential to empower women as they became economically empowered through the success of their businesses. A new look at the work of rural women, scaling innovations, linking them with the knowledge economy and focusing on equity, microfinance may likely to create social capital by promoting horizontal and vertical networks within a community, established by newer norms and social trust.

Through microfinance women have obtained equal control over resources and decision-making power. This is also a result of flexible gender relations which made it possible for women to be economically empowered through successful business initiatives, ownership, and profit/income in their hand, women also faced less difficulties in turning their economic empowerment into the overall empowerment in social, business, and political setting.

Adieu to Rural Indebtedness

One of the reasons for people in rural areas to be poor is their hereditary indebtness. It may sound weird but it is true fact that rural indebtness is an indicator of weak financial infrastructures of our country, which includes inability of our economic system to reach to the needy farmers, landless people in the villages and the agricultural wage labors. Thankfully microfinance has given a chance to come out of the indebtness, by creating own source of income.

Leadership Qualities

Women empowerment relates to leadership and recognition within the community. The practice of the group of rotating leadership has proved to be a positive factor in building confidence of members.

Self-Confidence

Self-confidence is one of the most crucial areas of change for empowerment, yet it is also one of the most difficult factors to measure or assess. Self-confidence is a complex concept relating to both women's perception of their capabilities and their actual level of skills and capabilities.

It's not about the income what the women generated out of the help of microfinance but the outlook to access a problem and attain its solution has changed the level of confidence of women. The confidence level of women related to SHGs represented 90 percent when compared to only 20 percent to women not related to SHGs

Intra-household Relations

Over the time, women's status undoubtedly has been improved in the society as well as in the family. Microfinance programmes have actually boosted the relationship of women. It's not only the loan facilitated by the microfinance institutions but also the savings worth of discussion. Access to credit and participation in income-generating activities is assumed to strengthen women's bargaining position within the household, thereby allowing her to influence a greater number of strategic decisions.

Decision-making

Microfinance institutions are finding ways to evaluate their impact on women's decision-making. The Centre for Self-Help Development (CSD) also reported that women were able to make small purchases of necessary items like groceries independently. This change in the village areas is remarkable, where most of the women are still illiterate.

Group Dynamism and Networking

It is more beneficial when women operate in a network because it is not just a louder voice but a strengthened workforce, better management, faster access and to summarize adds more gun powder to the equation. The success story of Lizzat Papad and how it succeeded is well known to all. It stands a testimony to how networking can be a solution to many problems of women entrepreneurs. Microfinance gave women such opportunities with much ease.

CONCLUSION

The confederation of women entrepreneurs (COWE) works on the democratic philosophy of "by the women, of the women and for the women" from various backgrounds aspiring to be socially, economically self reliant, irrespective of their present status provides guidance to grow and work as a group in a network

With the support of microfinance institutions or SHGs, the rural women now transformed their lives into full time and active entrepreneurs with lot of hope and are able to lead a life with self-esteem. Once the neglected part of the society and passive recipients of Government's doles, are active participants and stakeholders in different programmes women are now the leaders, decision-makers, managers, entrepreneurs and play all the other roles what they once thought to be dream. It is clearly visible that the women today are in a position where her intelligence and contribution is much seeked to develop the nation. Thus it can be said that microfinance has achieved its level best in putting small things in right place to bring a big change.

References

Ackerley, B. (1995), Testing the Tools of Development: Credit Programmes, Loan Involvement and Women's Empowerment, *World Development*, 26(3), 56-68.

Ahirrao, Jitendra (2009), "Rural Women Empowerment through Microfinance". *Kurukshetra*, Vol. 57, No. 4, February, 2009.

Batliwala, S. (1994), The Meaning of Women's Empowerment: New Concepts from Action

Dhavamani, P., Empowerment of Rural Women Through Self-Help Groups in Sattur Taluk of Virudhunagar District, *Journal for Bloomers of Research*, Vol. 2, No. 2, February 2010.

Joshi, S.C (2004), Women Empowerment: Myth and Reality, New Delhi, Akansha Publishing House.

Lalitha, K., "Impact of women empowerment and role of SHGs in value based emancipation", Vol. 1, Issue II, March 2011, pp. 130-33.

Kabeer, N. (2001), "Conflicts Over Credit: Re-evaluation the Empowerment Potential of Loans to Women in Rural Bangladesh": *World Development*, Vol. 29, No. 1.

Mayoux, L. (1998a), Women's Empowerment and Micro-finance programmes: Approaches, Evidence and Ways Forward. The Open University Working Paper No. 41.

Mayoux, Linda (1996), "The magic ingredient? Microfinance and women's empowerment'.'

Mayoux, Linda (2002), "Microfinance and women's empowerment: Rethinking best practice", *Development Bulletin*, No. 57, pp. 76-81.

Mayoux, Linda (2006), Women's Empowerment and Microfinance: A 'Think Piece' for the Microfinance Field, http://www.genfinance.info.

Tiyas Biswas (2008), Women Empowerment through Microfinance: A Boon for Development, *Social Welfare*, Vol. 8.

UNCDF Report.

The Hindu, 29-06-2006.

11

Microfinance: Socio-Economic and Cultural Changes Among Schedule Castes in Andhra Pradesh

Sree Vidya

INTRODUCTION

Rural women, in particular those belong to the economically and socially weaker sections of society have limited access to resources or employment opportunities that would make them financially independent. They survive in conditions that do not permit them to meet minimum consumption needs. Even the money earned by them from hard physical labor is not controlled by them. Institutional credit is difficult to access as women rarely have any property rights to mortgage or collateral to offer, and they have to depend on rural money-lenders for their production-*cum*-consumption needs. This entraps them into a vicious cycle of perpetual poverty and indebtedness.

Microfinance has evolved over the past quarter century across India into various operating forms and with varying degree of success. One such form of microfinance has been the development of the self-help movement. Based on the concept of "self-help," small groups of women have formed into groups of ten to twenty and operate a savings-first business model whereby the member's savings are used to furnish loans. The results from these self-help groups (SHGs) are promising and have become a focus of intense examination as it is proving to be an effective method of poverty reduction and bringing socio-cultural change, particularly among the marginalized communities.

A segment of Indian society hitherto known as 'Sudras' and 'Untouchables' that has suffered from social and economic disabilities, has come to be known as Scheduled castes in the present era. The term 'Scheduled Caste' is an expression standardized in the Constitution of India. In India, Dalit women constitute 80 million, 48 per cent of the total Dalit population and 16.3 per cent of the total female population. Above 81 per cent of Dalits live in rural areas.

Review of Literature

In the past few years many scientific studies on Scheduled Castes have been produced by various social scientists. A survey of review of literature has been presented in detail.

A brief account on the origin of Scheduled castes like "Mala" and "Madiga" are presented by Thurston (1909) and G.S. Gherye (1961), etc. In fact they have written monographs on the basis of Census records and official documents. A study of 72 SHGs undertaken by Harper *et al.*, (1998)—covering over 1,000 SHG members in Orissa, Uttar Pradesh, Maharashtra and Karnataka-too registered improvement in members' diet, assets and education. Linch (1969), while dealing with political assertion of Jatavs of Agra describes the aspirations and attempts for social mobility. Patwardhan (1973), Sachidananda (1977) and Malik (1979), discuss the social change among the Dalits in general, not considering any particular caste or castes. The studies that have relevance for the study include Cohn's study of Chamars in UP and Epstein's (1962) study of two villages in Mysore and Alexander's (1968) study of Pulayan and Palaya, Scheduled castes in Kerala.

Objectives of the Study

The main objectives of the study are:

- To examine the role of financial institutions in providing loans to the SHGs and income generation activities.
- To study the traces of socio-cultural changes that occurred due to participatory development, changing livelihoods and changes in levels of income.

Area and Sample

The area of the study consists of Krishna district in Andhra Pradesh and the focus is on its Scheduled Caste population. The unit of the sample is the member of woman self-help groups and her family belonging to Scheduled Castes in Krishna district. The sample was selected based on multi-stage random method.

Methodology

The data for the study were collected from both primary and secondary sources. The primary data were collected through anthropological field work using interview schedule, observation, formal and informal interviews and case study method. The secondary data collected from APRPRP, DRDA SC Corporation.

MICROFINANCE

The policy environment in India has been tremendously supportive of the growth of the microfinance sector. Particularly during the International Year of Microcredit, 2005, noteworthy policy announcements from the Government of India (GoI) and the Reserve Bank of India (RBI) have served as a shot in the arm for rapid expansion of this sector.

Self-Help Groups

Formation of Self-help groups among themselves shows that SCs try to identify themselves. From the gender point of view, the female population among the Scheduled castes suffers from specific disadvantages of caste, poverty, illiteracy and social isolation. There are specific areas in which the Scheduled caste women are particularly disadvantaged. The status of SC women was very poor before two decades. SHGs and Microfinance in recent times come to be recognized and accepted as one of the new development paradigms for alleviating poverty through social and economic empowerment of the poor particularly, women.

SHGs play a vital role in the Microfinance system. There have been perceptible and wholesome changes in the living standards of SHG members in terms of an increase in savings and borrowing capacity, income generating activities and income levels. The concept of savings, participation and interaction in the meetings, preparation of microcredit plan, access to financial institutions, starting income generation activities, marketing and increased income brought several changes within the individual, group and the community.

Sources of Loans

The District Rural Development Agency (DRDA) has been implementing 2 major Central schemes, i.e. Rural Poverty Reduction Project (RPRP) and Swarnajayanti Swarozgar Yojana (SGSY). Both are being implemented under the State scheme viz., Indira Kranthi Patham

(IKP). The sources of loans are Indira Kranthi patham (IKP), Banks, SC Corporation, DRDA/WDC/Government loans with Subsidies and Several Microfinance Institutions and Non-Governmental Organizations (NGOs).

The data reveal that the banks have provided 94.13 percent of the credit needs of the SHGs. The VOs and MS have provided negligible percent of loans to the SHGs. Similarly, the frequency of loans by banks constitutes 76.94 percent followed by SC corporation 20.22%. VOs and MS have only a negligible role in extending credit to the SHGs. However, they have organizational role in the development of SHGs.

Utilization of Loans

The consumption of large amount of loans reveals that the households are spending much on consumption expenditure on food, education, health, lifecycle rituals and other functions. The same expenditure pattern is observed across the study area. Mainly they spent the amount on Food materials and Health, Purchase of Agricultural units, or cattle purchase, asset creation, lifecycle rituals and education of children.

SOCIO-CULTURAL AND ECONOMIC CHANGES

The present paper presents the changes that in the economy and socio-cultural aspects of the SHG members and their families due to increased access to credit, asset creation, increase in income levels, access, exposure and participation in development activities institutions and attitudinal changes for better living among the SHG members.

Women play a pivotal role in the family and the community, shouldering all the responsibilities satisfying the needs of their spouses and children, running the households and managing within the limited budget. They provide services round the clock without any payment and yet they are considered economically dependent on their husband or any other male member of the family. In the rural areas, besides all the household responsibilities, bearing the children and bringing them up, they also work in the fields side by side with their men folk. It has certainly helped the people of different backgrounds to improve the socio-economic conditions and seek social status outside the pale of the traditional caste system. Besides, various development interventions particularly, SHGs and micro-finance have contributed much in bringing desired changes among the SCs. These facilitated the people including those whose economic and social mobility were restricted in the traditional system of stratification.

CHANGES IN ECONOMIC SPHERE

The SHGs and micro-finance provided opportunities to strengthen their existing occupation or to adopt new occupations. This makes them economically independent and often more choice in choosing the work they want to do. The government policies on land made some of them small landowners and sharecroppers. The use of technology in agriculture provided avenue to develop some skills in agriculture and its allied activities. The youth who were educated with the help of savings and credit of the SHG members got jobs in urban areas. Some of the SCs have improved their traditional skills by using new technology and becoming small entrepreneurs. The benefits of development programmes have also provided some avenues of self-employment, economic freedom and improved economic conditions. These get reflected and demonstrated in patterns of living, housing, social celebrations, etc.

Wealth Ranking

The study facilitated using PRA exercise (wealth ranking) to collect data on SHG members' households both before and after joining the SHGs by applying the objective wealth ranking technique. The households of SHG members are categorized in to five groups based on the wealth ranking indicators derived from the PRA exercise such as: (i) state of house; (ii) regulating of income; (iii) number of productive and household assets; (iv) degree of food security; (v) level of education; (vi) status of the health; (vii) others (include women headed households, poor physical and mental health, level of debt and alcoholism). All the sample households are classical into five categories such as: (i) very poor, (ii) poor, (iii) borderline, (iv) self-sufficient, and (v) surplus.

CHANGES IN SOCIAL SPHERE

Any assessment of the status of women has to start from the social framework. Social structure, cultural norms and value system influence social expectations regarding the behavior of men and women and determine a woman's role and her position in society to a great extent. The most important of these institutions are the systems of descent, family and kinship, marriage and religious traditions. They provide the ideology and moral basis, for men's and women's notions about their rights and duties. The normative standards do not change at the same pace as changes in other forms of social organizations brought about by such factors as technological and educational advance, urbanization, increasing population, and changing costs and standards of living.

The social status of Scheduled Caste women is a typical example of the gap between the position and role accorded to them by the Constitution and the laws, and those imposed on them by social traditions. What is possible for women in theory is seldom within their reach in fact.

Changes at Family Level

The SHGs and micro-finance brought changes in the size, structure, status, and role and inter relations of the family. The SC population follows the patrilineal mode of descent. The family is patriarchal in authority. The male domination is clear in decision-making. In the past most common family organization, the joint family, was composed of a group of patriarchal related males who have equal rights to property sharing a common budget, residence and hearth, though this pattern of living has been considerably affected by modernization, urbanization, and socio-economic changes. Women were placed under restrictions and have little or no say in decision-making and are directly subordinate to her mother-in-law. The data show that family is now mostly nuclear. Her status in the family depends greatly on her contribution to the family economy. At present both mother-in law and daughter in-law are the members of the same self help group, and they get loans from the banks individually for different purposes. In the present situation mother-in-laws, sister-in-laws and daughter-in-laws sharing the family burdens are helping each other. Scheduled Caste women in the field explore that decision-making in children's marriage, education, and in occupational change.

Among the Scheduled Castes there was a practice of bride-price in the past. This system changes to dowry due to education, employment and culture contact. Scheduled Castes practice this dowry system to show their status. In some cases SHG women take the loans and spend towards dowry for her children's marriage. With the awareness of importance of education to the girl child, parents among the Scheduled castes spent the amount equally on their children irrespective of gender bias. In the past Scheduled castes encourages early marriages of both male and female children, mostly above 15 and below the age of 18 years. Now, the age at marriage of both male and female is between 18 and 25 years. The delay in marriage is due to his/her education. The majority of the youth concentrates on their education, employment and well settled life. There is a practice of Widow Remarriage.

There are changes in interpersonal relations in the family. The savings, increased capacity in getting credit and income through SHG, the status and role of woman are enhanced in the family. She is getting more 'say' in family affairs and her relations with other members of the family become more cordial. The women began slowly participating in decision-making and financial management of their families. The children are admitted in private schools for better education. With the experiences acquired from the SHGs, the women become capable of interacting with PIAs in getting benefits from the government.

Changes at Community Level

The SHG members are capable of interacting with outsiders including officials and non-officials in dealing with the implementation of different rural development schemes at village and community levels. Their status and role are enhanced even at village and community levels. The Scheduled Castes traditionally occupied the lowest social position in the social hierarchy; they were kept away from the higher castes, and were considered as untouchables. The study reveals that particularly, Scheduled Caste women joined SHGs with other caste women. Those SHGs are called mixed groups. The SC women come to the main village to participate in General body meetings of the SHGs. It was also observed that in some of the villages Scheduled Caste women were unanimously elected as office bearers and executive members like President, Secretary and Treasurer, etc. in Village Organization. It shows that the social distance in the villages appears to be decreasing with the changing standard of life including food habits. Even in the rural areas where the stigma of untouchability prevailed, some of the people belonging to higher castes are providing food in their utensils and allowing them to dine along with them. This indicates that the practice of untouchbility and social distance is being reduced. They are changing their pattern of behavior and life styles including dress, housing, food habits and apparently less identifiable as a separate segment.

CHANGES IN POLITICAL SPHERE

Women constitute one half of the total population, but are denied the equal share in active politics of the country. In politics the organizational structure, leadership and shifting of power in government are mostly dominated by men. The money and caste are important factors which play the main role in Indian politics. Women's participation in the political process is centered around their struggle against oppression. The socio-economic status of women directly depends on their participation in the decision-making process.

In the political dimension, at places they have achieved power positions at the local level. They are members of the local bodies by virtue of reservation. A competition among them has formed and vertical divisions among the castes and their votes are important to all political candidates. This has given rise to increased demand from the government and the competing candidates. In these processes the quality of their participation and their self- confidence has increased.

CHANGES IN RELIGIOUS SPHERE

The religious traditions have a deep bearing on the role and changing status of the women. In the present study Scheduled castes followed two religions viz. Hinduism, and Christianity. Scheduled Castes in the past, and many of them in the present, follow the rituals of Hindus associated with religion. The impurity associated with menstruation and childbirth, restricts the women from joining in religious ceremonies. After marriage women perform special rituals for the well-being of their husbands and children.

Christianity was the tremendous and radical change among the Scheduled castes in the district. In their words, Hindus treat them like slaves and untouchables whereas Christianity show the path of equality of all people.

The increase in levels of income and easy access to credit make the SHG members belonging to both Hinduism and Christianity to spend more on socio-cultural rituals and to elevate their social status at the local community level. The data reveal that the average annual expenditure among the Hindus before becoming the members of SHGs was Rs. 1,02,000 and now this is increased to Rs. 2,93,000. Similarly, the Christians used to spend Rs. 1,36,700 per annum and it is increased to Rs. 3,99,500. Most of the converts celebrate both Christian and some of the Hindu festivals. The converts used to spend Rs. 23,200 on Hindu festivals and now it is increased to Rs. 51,700 per annum. This clearly shows that the SHG members are capable of spending more on festivals and the rituals associated from birth to death of an individual in order to elevate their social status and to expose their status in the community and the society at large.

Material Culture 'and Development

Culture includes both material and non-material aspects of life. There are clear indications of change in the material culture of the SHG members. Most of the SHG members possess better housing, household gadgets, and food, dress and dress patterns. Most of the houses are permanent and semi-permanent in the structure. Most of them possess television and furniture in their houses. Some they have refrigerators and telephone facility. However, most of them have mobile phones depending on their nature of the job. After becoming the members of SHGs, most of them left the conventional method of cooking and using LPG Stoves, cookers and modern utensils. Thatched huts which were their only type of houses in the past have vanished to a great extent. Houses with RCC roof are in majority followed by a few tiled houses.

In the past SC people used to believe in superstitions and most of them treated their diseases using folk ways of curing diseases. After getting education, awareness programmes and increased income, the SHG members started treating their diseases using modern medicine. Now they are going to hospitals and aware of all development programs relating to health.

CONCLUSION

The term 'Scheduled Caste' is Constitutional and not a sociological concept. Socially, the only thing they have shared in common is poverty and social disabilities. Women are critical factors in the process of moving their families out of poverty. Women need to be viewed not as beneficiaries but as an active participant in the process of development and change. Empowerment of women can be effectively achieved if poor women could be organized into groups—for community participation as well as the assertion of their rights in various services related to their economic and social well-being.

The rise of SHGs and microfinance made the women belonging to SCs to resort to habitual savings and to have easy access to credit. Microfinance is seen as part of integrated programmes for poverty reduction. The consumption of large amount of loans reveals that the households are spending much on consumption expenditure such as expenditure on food, education, health, lifecycle rituals and other functions. It emerges that the poor borrow small loans frequently for consumption purposes and large loans for production and asset creation and income generating activities.

The Constitutional provisions, land distribution, participation in democratic processes, State programmes for economic development and reservation in jobs act as a concomitant accelerating factors and processes for bringing social mobility and change among the Scheduled castes. The new awareness in all these processes has also generated the occasion for the SCs to organize and assert themselves. Thus a holistic, historical perspective appears to have relevance in comprehending the change. The process of Sanskritization, westernization, secular reference group model appear relevant in conceptualizing the emerging patterns of social change among the Scheduled castes in the study area.

Finally, changes may take place in social system, such as changes in the system of communication due to technological innovations. Social change among the SHG members has been analyzed and presented in four dimensions such as economic, social, political and cultural.

References

ADB, 1997: Micro-enterprise Development: Not by Credit Alone, Asian Development Bank. www.adb.org.

Alexander, 1968: Social Mobility in Kerala, Poona, Deccan College.

Almelu, 2008: "Group Formation—Modalities and Objectives", *Encyclopedia of Gender Equality and Development*, Vol. 1, edited by C.P. Yadav, Anmol publications Pvt. Ltd., New Delhi.

Amartya Sen, 2000: Social Exclusion: Concepts, Applications and Security", Asian Development Bank.

Epstein, T.S., 1962: "Economic Development and Social Change in South India", The English Language Book Society and Manchester University Press.

Fisher, T. and Sriram, M.S., 2002: Beyond Microcredit: Putting Development Bank into Microfinance, Vistar, New Delhi.

Ghurye., G.S., 1950: "Caste and Class in India", The Popular Book Depot, Bombay.

J.K. Pundir, 1997: Changing Patterns of Scheduled Castes: Rawat Publication, Jaipur.

Malik, 1979: The Integration of Scheduled Castes, Abhinav Publication, New Delhi.

Rao, V.M., 2003: Women Self-Help Groups, Profiles from Andhra Pradesh and Karnataka, *Kurukshetra*, Vol. 50, No. 6.

Sachidananda, 1977: "Harijan Elites", Thomson Press, Faridabad.

Srinivas, M.N., 1966: Social Change in Modern India. University of California Press, Berkeley.

Thurston, E., 1909: Castes and Tribes of Southern India, Madras Government Press, Cosmo Publication, Delhi.

12

Investment Choice of University Teachers: A Study

(With Special Reference to Teachers of Devi Ahilya Vishwa Vidyalaya, Indore)

DR. MANISH SITLANI

INTRODUCTION AND RATIONALE

Behavioral finance is one of the accelerating areas in developing countries including India. The basic factors behind this include excellent economic growth in these countries, which in turn has resulted in a corresponding rise in individual income level. The beginning of the globalization process in early nineties opened a new gateway for economic development in these countries. The availability of a large number of prospective customers in these countries made them target markets for major global players. This, supported by reforms measures undertaken by these countries, proved to be a boon for the masses in general, and for the middle-income group in specific. On one hand, this class is benefited with excellent employment opportunities at a local and global level, and on the other hand, growing economies have resulted in a manifold rise in individual income level. This has resulted in a sudden growth in household savings and investment.

The academicians in higher learning institutes, including university teachers, are privileged to educate the masses and are hence assumed to be more information sensitive or what is termed as 'rationale' while taking various decisions including investment decisions. The growing financial markets have provided an excellent opportunity for this segment of individuals to reap the benefits by standing on the platform of their 'pro-information personality'. This makes the relevance of demography for teachers in universities an interesting area to study. This paper has attempted to study the association of individualistic and profession-related demographics with investment choice of teachers of Devi Ahilya University, Indore.

Most of the modern financial theories are based on the idea that an investor takes careful account of all available information before making investment decisions. But much evidence is available that it is not the case. The analysis of investors' psychology is having a growing impact on investment research and practice as it seeks to expose and explain the shortcomings of modern financial theory.

The purpose of this research is to examine the association of individualistic and profession-related demographics with investment choice of teachers of Devi Ahilya University, Indore. Teachers imparting higher education are expected to carry a better understanding and interpretation of information, including financial information having forbearance on risk and return associated with the various investment avenues, as they are associated with a profession involved in developing and/or transferring knowledge to those lacking this. So, does that mean that, as against general individuals, demographic factors affect those imparting higher education in a different manner? Or looking it from the other side, do the teachers of higher education take investment decisions based on their ability to assess information and hence are not affected by individualistic demographic factors? This paper has explored the association between individualistic and profession-related demographic factors and investment choice of teachers of Devi Ahilya University, Indore.

LITERATURE SURVEY

Researchers and practitioners have suggested that demographic factors can be used to differentiate individuals in terms of their investment choice. The majority of the research conducted in the area of behavioral finance has attempted to explore the role of demographic variables on investment behavior of individuals. The focus has been on various demographic characteristics such as gender, age, marital status, profession, income, and education and finance specific knowledge.

A large number of researches have been undertaken to document the investment behavior of individuals [see Odean (1998) and Shu *et al.* (2005)]. There also exist evidences in the existing literature that suggests that individuals tend to reduce the amount of efforts involved in decision-making as the decision grows more complex [see Payne *et. al.* (1984)]. Further, researchers have also attempted to categorize individual investment strategies using empirical evidences [see Ng and Wu (2006) and Feng and Seasholes (2007)]. Extending this, other researchers have explored the factors affecting individuals' investment behavior [Lewellen *et al.* (1977), Bajtelsmit and Bernasek (1996) and Kover (1999)].

A large number of researchers including Bajtelsmit and Bernasek (1996), Jianakoplos and Bernasek (1998), and Grable (2000) could explore in their studies that females have a comparatively lower preference for risk than males. Contradictory were the findings explored by researchers like Hanna and Chen (1997) who, in their research work, concluded that gender is not significant in predicting financial risk tolerance of individuals. Powell and Ansic (1997) also explored that in spite of differences among men and women respondents in terms of risk tolerance and financial strategies, there exist no differences between them in terms of ability of performance in financial decision-making.

A large number of researchers including McInish (1982) and Palsson (1996) have explored that risk tolerance of an individual increases with age. Brown (1990) has a very interesting submission in this regard. They suggested that biological changes in enzymes due to the aging process may be responsible for change in risk tolerance of individuals. However, researches in recent time [see Grable and Joo (1997)] have failed to explore any association between age of individual investors and their financial risk tolerance and investment choice.

Some of the researchers like Roszkowski *et al.* (1993) have confirmed that single investors are comparatively more risk tolerant. On the contrary, researchers like McInish (1982), Masters (1989) and Haliassos and Bertaut (1995) found that there exist no significant relationship between marital status and risk tolerance/investment choice of individual investors.

There also exist empirical findings in the related literature evidencing a positive relationship between level of income/wealth and risk tolerance of an individual. Friedman (1957), Riley and Chow (1992), Grable and Lytton (1999) have explored the similar findings in their research works.

Increased education is assumed to increase the risk tolerance of individuals. This is because of the fact that education enables the person to assess risk more accurately and hence gain out of riskier decisions. Similar are the findings of researchers like Baker and Haslem (1974). and Sung and Hanna (1996).

A large number of researchers have found that level of information/knowledge and experience that an individual possess, have forbearance on the risk tolerance and investment choice one have. Dynan *et al.* (2004) explored that the risk taking differences between both genders soothe significantly when knowledge of financial markets and investments is considered.

Despite of the widespread popular acceptance of the ideas thrown up by behavioral finance, it is unusual to observe the relatively small amount of academic research examining impact of demography on investment choice especially considering highly educated investors. As far as work done on university teachers in Indore is concerned, the researcher could not find any related literary work.

RESEARCH QUESTION AND OBJECTIVES

What is the Investment Choice of teachers of Devi Ahilya University, Indore and is it associated with their individualistic and/or profession-related Demographic Variables?

The objectives of this study are:

- To study the Investment Choice of teachers of Devi Ahilya University, Indore.
- To explore the association between individualistic and profession-related Demographic Variables and Investment Choice of teachers of Devi Ahilya University, Indore.

HYPOTHESES

A number of researches have shown that investment choice is affected by various demographic factors associated with individuals. The target population of this research work is teachers of Devi Ahilya University, Indore, who are assumed to have relatively higher level of education as generally they all are qualified post-graduation and above, hence are expected to behave rationally irrespective of various demographic factors viz. gender, age, marital status, nature of occupation, household income, qualification. Apart from the general demographic variables including gender, age, qualification, household income, marital status, existing wealth and investment experience, profession specific demography of respondents including the designation and area of specialization have also been considered for the purpose of this study. The basic proposition underlying this research work is that university teachers, like other individuals, are affected by general individual demography and there is no association of their profession-related demography with their investment choice. So we hypnotize that:

H1: There is a significant association between Gender and

Investment Choice of teachers of Devi Ahilya University, Indore.

H2: There is a significant association between Age and Investment Choice of teachers of Devi Ahilya University, Indore.

H3: There is a significant association between Marital Status and Investment Choice of teachers of Devi Ahilya University, Indore.

H4: There is a significant association between household income and Investment Choice of teachers of Devi Ahilya University, Indore.

H5: There is a significant association between qualification and Investment Choice of teachers of Devi Ahilya University, Indore.

H6: There is a significant association between Existing Wealth and Investment Choice of teachers of Devi Ahilya University, Indore.

H7: There is a significant association between Investment Experience and Investment Choice of teachers of Devi Ahilya University, Indore.

H8: There is no significant association between Designation and Investment Choice of teachers of Devi Ahilya University, Indore.

H9: There is no significant association between Area of Specialization and Investment Choice of teachers of Devi Ahilya University, Indore.

RESEARCH METHODOLOGY

An empirical investigation of Investment Choice of teachers of Devi Ahilya University, Indore is undertaken. An attempt has been made to explore the association between Investment Choice and various individualistic and profession-related demographic factors of teachers of Devi Ahilya University, Indore. In order to explore the Investment Choice of teachers of Devi Ahilya University, Indore, a self-structured questionnaire with close-ended options was instituted on respondents. Thereafter, the Chi-square test has been applied to determine the association between Investment Choice (dependent variable) and various individualistic and profession-related demographic factors (independent variables).

The study is exploratory in nature. For this purpose, the researchers have classified all the available investment avenues in five categories based on a closed group discussion among finance professionals and academicians. These categories are: 1. Equities and

Derivatives, 2. Mutual fund and insurance, 3. Fixed return investments, 4. Real estate, and 5. Gold and Bullion. Demographic variables considered for the study are Gender, Age, Marital Status, Annual Household Income, Qualification, Existing Wealth, Investment Experience, Designation and Area of Specialization.

The universe of this study include all the on roll (regular) teachers teaching in different courses at various university teaching departments (UTDs) of Devi Ahilya University, Indore. There are around 30 teaching departments in Devi Ahilya University, Indore and approximately 300 teachers are working in these departments including approx. 60 professors, more than 60 Readers/Lecturers (Selection Grade) and more then 155 Lecturers/Senior Lecturers. The Sampling method used can best be described as a mix of Quota and Judgmental Sampling. The data was collected through a self-structured questionnaire, which was administered during the month of April-May 2010 on 90 respondents. The quota was fixed approximately @ 30% teachers from each department. Thereafter, the researchers used their judgment to select respondents in order to cover all demographic variables. The analysis of the data was carried out using Statistical Package for the Social Sciences (SPSS) for Windows.

ANALYSIS

Table 1 gives the summary of demographic characteristics of the respondents. The respondents were asked to give relative ranks to five investment choices, one being most preferred and five being least preferred. The mean ranks of their investment choice and other relevant statistics is shown in Table 2.

The Table 2A below exhibits the relative preference of an investment choice from the point of view of all the respondents. The table shows that the mean value of the preference/rank given to 'Mutual Funds and Insurance' is 2.24, which is least among the five choices given to respondents. It employs that 'Mutual Funds and Insurance' is the most preferred investment choice of respondents. This is followed by 'Fixed Return Investments', 'Gold and Bullion' and 'Equity and Derivatives' with a mean score of 2.81, 3.26 and 3.26 respectively. The respondents seem to be almost indifferent in their preferences for 'Gold and Bullion' and 'Equity and Derivatives', as the mean ranks for these two options are same with a small difference in standard deviation. 'Real Estate' is being explored as the least preferred choice of respondents with a mean score of 3.43.

The Table 2B exhibits the frequency of respondents ranking the various investment avenues as their most preferred investment choice. A maximum of 28 respondents has ranked 'Fixed Return Investments' as

TABLE I

Demographic Characteristics of Respondents

Variable	*Frequency*	*Percentage*
Gender		
Female	49	54.40
Male	41	45.60
Age		
> 30 yrs.	20	22.20
30+ yrs. to 40 yrs.	39	43.30
40+ yrs. to 50 yrs.	16	17.80
More than 50 yrs.	15	16.70
Marital Status		
Married	69	76.70
Single	21	23.30
Household Income (Rs.)		
Less than 4 Lacs	38	42.20
4 Lac to 8 Lacs	40	44.40
More than 8 Lacs	12	13.30
Qualification		
Post-graduate	37	41.10
Post-graduate with Ph.D.	24	26.10
Post-graduate with Professional Degree	20	22.20
PG with Ph.D. and Professional Degree	9	10.00
Present Wealth (Rs.)		
Less than 1 Lac	34	37.80
1 Lac to 5 Lacs	40	44.40
More than 5 Lacs	16	17.80
Equity Investment Experience		
Yes	25	27.80
No	65	72.20
Designation		
Lecturer/Senior Lecturer	54	60.00
Reader/Lecturer (Selection Grade)	22	24.40
Professor	14	15.60
Area of Specialization		
Finance/Accounts/Economics	29	32.20
Others	61	67.80

their most preferred investment choice, followed by 22 respondents ranking for 'Mutual Funds and Insurance' as their most preferred choice. An equal number of 14 respondents each have ranked 'Real Estate' and 'Equity and Derivatives' as their most preferred choice, while only a minimum of 12 respondents has ranked 'Gold and Bullion' as their most preferred investment choice.

Table 2A
Descriptive Statistics

Investment Avenue	*N*	*Min.*	*Maxi.*	*Mean*	*Std. Dev.*	*Rank*
Equities and Derivatives	90	1	5	3.26	1.37850	4
Mutual fund and insurance	90	1	5	2.24	0.92786	1
Fixed return investments	90	1	5	2.81	1.56431	2
Real estate	90	1	5	3.43	1.46149	5
Gold and Bullion	90	1	5	3.26	1.35382	3

Table 2B
Frequency Table for Ranks Allotted by University Teachers

Investment Option Rank Allotted	*Equity & Derivatives*	*Mutual Fund & Insurance*	*Fixed Ret. Investments*	*Real Estate*	*Gold & Bullion*
1	14	22	28	14	12
2	13	32	16	13	16
3	20	28	10	12	20
4	22	08	17	22	21
5	21	00	19	29	21
Total	90	90	90	90	90

The prime objective of the study is to explore the association between demographic variables of university teachers of Indore and their Investment Choice. The hypotheses of the study have been tested with the help of chi-square performed with the help of SPSS software. The hypotheses have been tested at 5% significance level.

Association between Gender and Investment Choice

As seen from Table 3 below, a maximum of 38.8% of female respondents have ranked 'Fixed Return Investments' as their most preferred investment choice, while a maximum of 31.7% of males has

Table 3
Cross-Tabulation and Chi-square values for Gender and Investment Choice

Investment Preference →		*Equity & Derivatives*	*Mutual Funds & Insurance*	*Fixed Return Investment*	*Real Estate*	*Gold & Bullion*	*Total*
Female	Count	4	13	19	1	12	49
	%	8.2	26.5	**38.8**	**2**	24.5	**100.0%**
Male	Count	10	9	9	13	0	41
	%	24.4	22	22	**31.7**	**0**	**100.0%**
Pearson Chi-Square				Value	df	Asymp. Sig. (2-sided)	
				28.671	4	.000	

ranked 'Real Estate' as their first preference, which is the least preferred investment choice for females as only 2% females have ranked it to be their most preferred investment choice. As far as males are concerned, 'Gold and Bullion' have arrived as least preferred investment choice as none of the males have ranked it to be their preferred investment choice. So, what has appeared as the most preferred investment choice for 'Male' respondents' has contrarily appeared as the least preferred investment choice for 'Female' respondents. So, there seems to be no significant association between Gender and Investment Choice of respondents.

A close look into chi-square value of 28.671 with a significance level of .000 reveals that there is a significant association between Gender and Investment Choice. Hence, the null hypothesis H1 "*There is a significant association between Gender and Investment Choice of teachers of Devi Ahilya University, Indore.*" is not rejected.

Association between Age and Investment Choice

On the basis of age, the respondents have been classified in four age categories viz. 'Less than 30 years', '30 years to 40 years', '40 years to 50 years', and 'More than 50 years'. As seen from Table 4, the maximum of 35% of the respondent university teachers in the youngest age group (less than 30 years) has ranked 'Equity and Derivatives' as their most preferred investment choice, while none of this group of respondents has ranked 'Real Estate' as their most preferred investment choice. Respondents in next two age categories (30 years to 40 years, 40 years to 50 years) have ranked Fixed Return Investments as their most preferred investment choice. For respondents in the age group of '30 years to 40 years', 'Equity and derivatives' is the least preferred investment choice, and for respondents in the age group of '40 years to

TABLE 4

Cross-Tabulation and Chi-square Values for Age and Investment Choice

Investment Preference →		*Equity & Derivatives*	*Mutual Funds & Insurance*	*Fixed Return Investments*	*Real Estate*	*Gold & Bullion*	*Total*
Less then 30 yrs.	Count	7	3	6	0	4	20
	%	**35**	15	30	**0**	20	100.0%
30 yrs. to 40 yrs.	Count	1	11	15	5	7	39
	%	**2.6**	28.2	**38.5**	12.8	17.9	100.0%
40+ yrs. to 50 yrs.	Count	2	3	6	5	0	16
	%	12.5	18.8	**37.5**	31.3	**0**	100.0%
Above 50 yrs.	Count	4	5	1	4	1	15
	%	26.7	**33.3**	**6.7**	26.7	**6.7**	100.0%
Pearson Chi-Square				Value	df	Asymp. Sig. (2-sided)	
				26.753	12	.008	

50 years', 'Gold and Bullion' is their least preferred investment choice (0%). As far as respondents in the age group of 50 years and above are concerned, 'Mutual Funds and Insurance' is their most preferred investment choice, with 33.3% respondents ranking for it.

The Chi-square table above is showing a Chi-square value of 26.753 with a significance level of .008, which indicates that there is a significant association between age and investment choice. Hence, null hypothesis H2, *"There is a significant association between Age and Investment Choice of teachers of Devi Ahilya University, Indore"* is not rejected.

Association between Marital Status and Investment Choice

On the basis of marital status, the respondents have been classified as 'Married' and 'Single'. As seen from Table 5, the majority of the 'Married' respondents (33.33%) has ranked 'Fixed Return Investments' as their most preferred investment choice. 'Gold and Bullion' is their least preferred investment choice of these respondents, which, on the contrary, has appeared as most preferred investment choice for respondents in 'Single' category. For 'Single' respondents, 'Real Estate' is their least preferred investment choice. Again, there seems to be a significant association between Marital Status and Investment Choice of teachers of Devi Ahilya University, Indore.

TABLE 5

Cross-Tabulation and Chi-square Values for Marital Status and Investment Choice

Investment Preference →		*Equity & Derivatives*	*Mutual Funds & Insuran ce*	*Fixed Return Investment*	*Real Estate*	*Gold & Bullion*	*Total*
Married	Count	9	19	23	13	5	69
	%	13	27.5	**33.3**	18.8	**7.2**	100.0%
Single	Count	5	3	5	1	7	21
	%	23.8	14.3	23.8	**4.8**	**33.3**	100.0%
Pearson Chi-Square				Value	df	Asymp. Sig. (2 -sided)	
				13.094	4	.011	

The Chi-square value of 13.094 with a significance level of .011 reveals that there is a significant association between Marital Status and Investment Choice of respondents. Hence, the null hypothesis H3: *"There is a significant association between Marital Status and Investment Choice of teachers of Devi Ahilya University, Indore"* is not rejected.

Association between Household Income and Investment Choice

On the basis of household income respondents were divided into three sub-groups. As seen from Table 6, maximum respondents with household income of 'Less than 4 Lac Rs.' (52.6%) have ranked 'Fixed

Return Investments' as their most preferred investment choice, while for respondents with household income of 'Rs. 4 Lacs to Rs. 8 Lacs', 'Mutual Funds and Insurance' is the most preferred investment choice (35%). As far as respondents in the last household income category of 'More then Rs. 8 Lacs' is concerned, 'Equities and Derivatives' is their most preferred investment choice. All the sample sub-groups also differ considerably in respect of their least preferred investment choice. So, there seems to be an association between Household Income and Investment Choice of teachers of Devi Ahilya University, Indore.

TABLE 6

Cross Tabulation and Chi-square Values for Household Income and Most Preferred Investment Choice

Investment Preference →		*Equity & Derivatives*	*Mutual Funds & Insurance*	*Fixed Return Investment*	*Real Estate*	*Gold & Bullion*	*Total*
Upto Rs. 4 Lacs	Count	3	7	20	5	3	38
	%	7.9	18.4	**52.6**	13.2	7.9	100.0%
Rs. 4 Lacs + to Rs. 8 Lacs	Count	7	14	6	6	7	40
	%	17.5	**35**	15	15	17.5	100.0%
More than Rs. 8 Lacs	Count	4	1	2	3	2	12
	%	**33.3**	8.3	16.7	25	16.7	100.0%
Pearson Chi-Square				Value	df	Asymp. Sig. (2 -sided)	
				19.730	8	.011	

The Chi-square Table 6 shows that chi-square value for association between Household Income and Investment Choice is 19.730 with an assumptive significance of .011. This represents that there is a significant association between Household Income of teachers of Devi Ahilya University, Indore and their Investment Choice. Hence, the null hypothesis H4 *"There is a significant association between Household Income and Investment Choice of teachers of Devi Ahilya University, Indore"* is not rejected.

Association between Qualification and Investment Choice

On the basis of qualification, respondents were classified as 'Post-graduate', 'Post-graduate with Ph.D.', 'Post-graduate with Professional Degree' and 'Post-graduate with Ph.D. and Professional Degree'. As shown in Table 7, all the four sample sub-groups have shown different priorities for their most preferred investment choice. While 'Post-graduate' respondents have ranked 'Fixed Return Investments as their most preferred investment choice' (51.4%), respondents with 'Post-graduate and Ph.D.' qualification have equally ranked 'Equity and Derivatives' and 'Real Estate' as their most preferred investment choice (25% each). On the other hand, a maximum of 35% of respondents with 'Post-graduation and professional qualification' have ranked 'Gold and Bullion' as their most preferred investment choice, and differing from these respondents in the highest qualification category have preferred 'Mutual Funds and Insurance' as their investment choice (55.6%). The respondents in various sample sub-groups also seem to differ in terms of their least preferred investment choice.

TABLE 7

Cross-Tabulation and Chi-square Values for Qualification and Most Preferred Investment Choice

Investment Preference →		*Equity & Derivatives*	*Mutual Funds & Insurance*	*Fixed Return Investment*	*Real Estate*	*Gold & Bullion*	*Total*
Post-graduate	Count	4	8	19	3	3	**37**
	%	10.8	21.6	**51.4**	8.1	8.1	100.0%
Post-graduate & Ph.D.	Count	6	5	5	6	2	24
	%	**25**	20.8	20.8	**25**	8.3	100.0%
Post-graduate & Professional Degree	Count	3	4	4	2	7	20
	%	15	20	20	10	**35**	100.0%
Post-graduate with Ph.D. & Professional Degree	Count	1	5	0	3	0	9
	%	11.1	**55.6**	0	33.3	11.1	100.0%
Pearson Chi-Square			Value		df	Asymp. Sig. (2 -sided)	
			29.655		12	.003	

The table above shows that chi-square value for association between Qualification and Investment Choice is 29.655 with an assumptive significance of .003. This represents that there is a significant association between Qualification of teachers of Devi Ahilya University, Indore and their Investment Choice Category. Hence, the null hypothesis H5: *"There is a significant association between Qualification and Investment Choice of teachers of Devi Ahilya University, Indore"* is not rejected.

Association between Existing Wealth and Investment Choice

On the basis of Existing Wealth, respondents were divided in three sample sub-groups. Table 8 shows that for first two sample sub-groups with existing wealth of 'Less than Rs. 1 Lac' and Rs. '1 Lac to Rs. 5 Lacs' respectively, the majority of respondents has ranked 'Fixed Return Investments' as their most preferred investment choice. On the other hand, respondents with existing wealth of 'More than Rs. 5 Lacs' have ranked 'Mutual Funds and Insurance' as their most preferred investment choice. Thus, on the basis of existing wealth, respondents seem to be quite different in terms of their investment choice.

The Chi-square value for association between Existing Wealth and Investment Choice is 16.751 with an assumptive significance of .033. This represents that there is a significant association between Existing Wealth of teachers of Devi Ahilya University, Indore and their Investment Choice. Hence, the null hypothesis H6: *"There is a significant association between Existing Wealth and Investment Choice of teachers of Devi Ahilya University, Indore"* is not rejected.

TABLE 8

Cross-Tabulation and Chi-square Values for Existing Wealth and Most Preferred Investment Choice

Investment Preference	→	*Equity & Derivatives*	*Mutual Funds & Insur ance*	*Fixed Return Investment*	*Real Estate*	*Gold & Bullion*	*Total*
Less then Rs. 1 Lac	Count	3	7	16	4	4	34
	%	8.8	20.6	**47.1**	11.8	11.8	100.0%
Rs. 1 Lac to Rs. 5 Lacs	Count	7	7	12	7	7	40
	%	17.5	17.5	**30**	17.5	17.5	100.0%
More than Rs. 5 Lacs	Count	4	8	0	3	1	16
	%	25	**50**	0	18.8	6.2	100.0%
Pearson Chi-Square			Value	df	Asymp. Sig. (2 -sided)		
			16.751	8	.033		

Association between Investment Experience and Investment Choice

On the basis of Investment Experience, the respondents were divided in two sample sub-groups,, i.e. 'With Investment Experience' and 'Without Investment Experience'. For the respondents in 'With Investment Experience' sample sub-group, the majority of respondents (56%) have ranked 'Equity and Derivatives' as their most preferred investment choice, whereas for the respondents in 'Without Investment Experience' sample sub-group, none of the respondents have ranked this investment avenue as their most preferred investment choice. For this category of the majority of respondents (41.5%), 'Fixed Return Investments' is their most preferred investment choice. So, there seems to be a significant association between Investment Experience and Investment Choice of University Teachers in Indore.

TABLE 9

Cross-Tabulation and Chi-square Values for Investment Experience and Most Preferred Investment Choice

Investment Preference	→	*Equity & Derivatives*	*Mutual Funds & Insurance*	*Fixed Return Investment*	*Real Estate*	*Gold & Bullion*	*Total*
With Equity Experience	Count	14	5	1	3	2	25
	%	**56**	20	4	12	8	100.0%
Without Equity Experience	Count	0	17	27	11	10	65
	%	0	26.2	**41.5**	16.9	15.4	100.0%
Pearson Chi-Square			Value		df	Asymp. Sig. (2- sided)	
			45.878		4	.000	

As seen from the Table 9 above, the Chi-square value for an association between Investment Experience and Investment Choice is 45.878 with assumptive significance of .000. This represents that there is a significant association between Investment Experience of teachers of Devi Ahilya University, Indore and their Investment Choice. Hence, the null hypothesis H7: "*There is a significant association between Investment Experience and Investment Choice of teachers of Devi Ahilya University, Indore*" is not rejected.

Association between Designation and Investment Choice

On the basis of designation, respondents were divided into three categories; 'Lecturers/Senior Lecturers', 'Readers/Lecturers (Selection Grade)', and 'Professors'. As seen from Table 10, respondents in the first sub-category of designation have ranked 'Fixed Return Investments' as their most preferred investment choice, followed by 'Mutual Funds and Insurance'. On the other hand, respondents in remaining two sub-categories have ranked 'Mutual Funds and Insurance' as their most preferred investment choice. All the respondent sub-groups in this category have indicated different investment avenues as their least preferred investment choice.

TABLE 10
Cross-Tabulation and Chi-square Values for Designation and Most Preferred Investment Choice

Table X: Cross Tabulation and Chi -square values for Designation and Most Preferred Investment Choice

Investment Preference	→	*Equity & Derivatives*	*Mutual Funds & Insurance*	*Fixed Return Investment*	*Real Estate*	*Gold & Bullion*	*Total*
Lecturer/Sr. Lecturer	Count	7	10	24	5	8	54
	%	13	18.5	**44.4**	9.3	14.8	100.0%
Reader/ Lecturer (SG)	Count	4	7	2	6	3	22
	%	18.2	**31.8**	9.1	27.3	13.6	100.0%
Professor	Count	3	5	2	3	1	14
	%	21.4	**35.7**	14.3	21.4	**7.1**	100.0%
Pearson Chi-Square			Value	df	Asymp. Sig. (2 -sided)		
			14.543	8	.069		

The Chi-square value shown by Table 10 for this association is 14.543 with a significance level of .069. This represents that there is no significant association between Designation of teachers of Devi Ahilya University, Indore and their Investment Choice at 5% significance level. Hence, the null hypothesis H8 "*There is no significant association between Designation and Investment Choice of teachers of Devi Ahilya University, Indore*" is not rejected.

Association between Area of Specialization and Investment Choice

As the teachers dealing with the area of Finance/Accounts/Economics are assumed to be more aware financially, the respondents were divided into two sub-groups as shown in Table 11. The respondents in 'Finance/Accounts/Economics' category are found to be most concentrated (41.4%) towards 'Mutual Funds and Insurance' as their most preferred Investment Choice, whereas a maximum of 37.7% of respondents in 'Others' category have ranked 'Fixed Return Investments' as their most preferred investment choice The two sample sub-groups also seem to differ in terms of their least preferred investment choice.

TABLE 11

Cross Tabulation and Chi-square Values for Area of Specialization and Most Preferred Investment Choice

Investment Preference	→	*Equity & Derivatives*	*Mutual Funds & Insurance*	*Fixed Return Investment*	*Real Estate*	*Gold & Bullion*	*Total*
Finance/ Accounts/ Economics	Count	5	12	5	3	4	29
	%	17.2	**41.4**	17.2	10.3	13.8	100.0%
Others	Count	9	10	23	11	8	61
	%	14.8	16.4	**37.7**	18	13.1	100.0%
Pearson Chi-Square				Value	df	Asymp. Sig. (2-sided)	
				8.497	4	.075	

The Chi-square value shown by the Table 11 for the aforesaid association is 8.497 with a significance level of .075. This represents that there is no significant association between Area of Specialization of teachers of Devi Ahilya University, Indore and their Investment Choice at 5% significance level. Hence, the null hypothesis H9: *"There is no significant association between Area of Specialization and Investment Choice of teachers of Devi Ahilya University, Indore"* is not rejected.

MAJOR FINDINGS

The major findings of this research work are summed up in following points:

- Gender, as in case of general individuals, has a significant association with investment choice of university teachers in Indore. While female university teachers in Indore are more inclined towards Fixed Return Investments, male teachers are inclined towards Real Estate.
- Age of university teachers in Indore is also found to be significantly associated with their investment choice. While younger teachers are more interested in Equity and Derivatives, older teachers are found to be more interested in Mutual Funds and Insurance. Teachers falling in between two extreme age groups are inclined towards Fixed Return Investments.
- Most of the married university teachers in Indore were found to be interested in investing in Fixed Return

Investments. On the other hand, single university teachers in Indore have shown an inclination for buying Gold and Bullion.

- With increasing household income, university teachers in Indore are found to be shifting towards riskier investment avenues, as those with lower household income were found to be inclined towards Fixed Return Investments, those with moderate household income were more interested in Mutual Funds and Insurance, and those with higher household income have preferred Equity and Derivatives as their investment choice.
- Though all respondents were highly qualified, qualification of respondent teachers of Devi Ahilya University, Indore was found to be significantly associated with their investment choice. Teachers with the bare minimum required qualification of post-graduation were interested in safer investment avenues like c. With increased qualifications, the investment choice was found to be concentrated towards Real Estate, Gold and Bullion and Mutual Funds and Insurance respectively.
- Even existing wealth of university teachers in Indore is found to be affecting their investment preference. While teachers with lower wealth of up to less than Rs. 5 Lacs were more interested in university teachers in Indore, teachers with existing wealth of Rs. 5 Lac and above have preferred investing in Mutual Funds and Insurance.
- Investment experience of university teachers in Indore is also found to be significantly associated with their investment choice. As expected, teachers with investment experience are more interested in investing in Equity and Derivatives, and on the other hand, teachers without investment experience were more interested in Fixed Return Investments.
- Profession related demographic traits like Designation and Area of Specialization of university teachers in Indore have no significant role to play in terms of their investment preference.

PRACTICAL IMPLICATIONS

The following points highlight the practical implications of this study:

- Investment choice of academicians in higher learning institutes in Indore like university teaching departments is not affected by profession-related demographic traits like the designation and area of specialization. So, those offering various investment avenues and other players in individual investment industry need not to focus on specific professional traits while dealing with their clients associated as teachers with higher learning institutes like university teaching departments in Indore.

- Even the specific segment of individuals like teachers associated with various teaching departments of Devi Ahilya University, Indore are affected by various individualistic demographic traits like Gender, Age, Marital Status, Household Income, Qualification, Existing Wealth and Investment Experience.
- University teachers in Indore, who are younger in age (less than 30 years), have a higher household income (of more than Rs. 8 Lacs) and carries investment experience may be offered riskier investment avenues like Equity and Derivatives, while those elder in age (more than 50 years) with higher existing wealth (of more than Rs. 5 Lacs) and moderate household income (in the range of Rs. 4 to 8 Lacs) may be offered investment avenues like Mutual Funds and Insurance.
- Married and Female university teachers in Indore, who falls in middle age brackets (of 30 to 50 years), have a comparatively lower qualification (PG only), have lower household incomes (upto Rs. 4 Lacs only), have low or moderate level of existing wealth (up to Rs. 5 Lacs only) and also does not carry any investment experience may be offered safer investment avenues like Fixed Return Investments.

CONCLUSION

Studies conducted by various academicians, research scholars and research organizations have evidenced that demographic variables have a significant association with the investment choice of individuals. These studies have proved that investors do not behave rationally and their choice of investment is decided by demographic factors like age, gender, income level, etc. On the contrary, there also exists a number of research works exploring the impact of rationality (in terms of financial knowledge, investment experience, etc.) on investment choice of individuals. These studies have proved that investors behave more rationally as their financial literacy/knowledge and experience increases.

The present study was conducted with a sample of 90 individual respondents from various teaching departments of Devi Ahilya University, Indore, who are reasonably considered knowledgeable as generally they all have a minimum post-graduation qualification. Further, being in an industry involved in imparting formal knowledge, they are expected to be more information interpretative. So, there exists an obvious doubt that whether or not this category of individuals are also governed by general individualistic demographic variables while making their investment choices, or their profession-related demography has some role to play? In order to know the same, an association of various individualistic and few profession-related demographic variables with investment choice was explored. It was observed that there is no significant association between profession-related demographic variable viz. 'Designation' and 'Area of Specialization', whereas there exists an significant association between all the individualistic demographic variables considered for the purpose of the study and Investment Choice of teachers of Devi Ahilya University, Indore.

References

Abdisalam Ali Ibrahim Rustam Rahmatovich Vosilov, 2008. Financial Investment Choice: differences between women and men, Bachelor's Thesis, Fall Semester 2008 Umeå School of Business Umeå University

Ajmi Jasim, 2008. Investment Choice of Individual Investors in an Emerging Market, *International Research Journal of Finance and Economics*, Issue 17

Bajtelsmit, V. and Bernasek, A., 1996. Why do women invest differently than men?, *Financial Counseling and Investing*, pp. 1-10.

Baker, H. and J. Haslem, 1974. The Impact of Investor Socioeconomic Characteristics on Risk and Return Preferences, *Journal of Business Research*, pp. 469-76.

Brown, D.P., 1990. Age clienteles induced by liquidity constraints, *International Economic Review*, pp. 891-912.

Chaulk Barbara, Johnson Phyllis and Bulcroft, 2003. Effects of Marriage and Children on financial Investment Choice: A Synthesis of Family development and Prospect Theory, *Journal of Family and Economic Issue*, Vol. 24(3).

Dynan Karen, Jonathan Skinner and Stephen Zeldes, 2004. Do The Rich Save More?, *Journal of Political Economy*, (April), pp. 397-444.

Feng, L. and Seasholes, M.S., 2007. Individual Investors and Gender Similarities in an Emerging Stock Market, *Pacific-Basin Finance Journal*, Online version.

Friedman Milton, 1957. "A Theory of The Consumption Function", Princeton University Press.

Grable, J.E., 2000. Financial risk tolerance and additional factors that affect risktaking in everyday money matters, *Journal of Business and Psychology*, pp. 625-30.

Grable, J.E., and Joo, S., 1997. Determinants of risk preference: implication for the family and consumer science professionals, *Family Economics and Resource Management Biennial*, pp. 19-24.

Grable, J.E. and Lytton, R.H., 1999. Investor risk tolerance: testing the efficiency of demographics as differentiating and classifying factors, *Financial Counsel and Planning*, pp. 61-74.

Haliassos, M. and Bertaut, C.C., 1995. Why do so few hold stocks?, *Economic Journal*, pp. 1110-29.

Hanna, S.D. and P. Chen, 1997. Subjective and Objective Risk Tolerance: Implications for Optimal Portfolio, *Financial Counselling and Planning*, pp. 17–26.

Harlow, W.V. and Keith Brown, 1990. Understanding and Assessing Financial Investment Choice: A Biological Perspective, *Financial Analysts Journal*, Vol. 46, pp. 50-62.

Jianakoplos, N.A. and Bernasek, A., 1998. Are Women More Risk Averse?, *Economic Enquiry*, pp. 620-30.

Kover, A., 1999. Okay, women really could use special advice about investing, *Fortune*, pp. 129-32.

Lewellen, W., Lease, R. and Schlarbaum, G., 1977. Patterns of investment strategy and behavior among individual investors, *Journal of Business*, pp. 296-333.

Masters, R., 1989. Study examines investors' risk-taking propensities, *Journal of Financial Planning*, July, pp. 151-55.

McInish, T.H., 1982. Individual investors and risk-taking, *Journal of Economic Psychology*, pp. 125-36.

Ng L. and Wu F., 2006. Revealed stock preferences of individual investors: Evidence from Chinese equity markets, *Pacific-Basin Finance Journal*, pp. 175-92.

Odean, T., 1998. Are investors reluctant to realize their losses?, *Journal of Finance*, pp. 1775–98.

Palsson, A.M., 1996. Does the Degree of Risk Aversion Vary With Household Characteristics, *Journal of Economic Psychology*, pp. 771-87.

Payne, J.W., Laughhunn, D.J. and Crum, R., 1984. Multiattribute risky choice behavior: The editing of complex prospects, *Management Science*, pp. 1350-61.

Powell, M. and Ansic, D., 1997. Gender differences in risk behavior in financial decision-making: an experimental analysis, *Journal of Economic Psychology*, pp. 605-28.

Riley, W.B. and Chow, K.V., 1992. Asset allocation and individual risk aversion, *Financial Analysts Journal*, Vol. 48, No. 6, pp. 32-37.

Roszkowski, M.J., Snelbecker, G.E. and Leimberg, S.R., 1993. Risk tolerance and risk aversion, The tools and techniques of financial planning, 4th ed., *National Underwriter*, Cincinnati, USA.

Rui Yao, Michael, S. Gutter, and Sherman, D. Hanna, 2005. The Financial Investment Choice of Blacks, Hispanics and Whites, *Financial Counseling and Planning*, Volume 16(1).

Scherman Diane, K. and Debra Drecnik Worden, 2003. Generation X: Understanding Their Investment Choice and Investment Behavior, *Journal of Financial Planning*, The Financial Planning Association, September 2003—Article 8.

13

Behavioral Finance: A New Perspective for Incorporating Investor Behavior in Portfolio Management

ATUL SHIVA AND MONICA SETHI

I. INTRODUCTION

Behavioral Finance combines behavior and cognitive psychology with conventional economics and finance to explain why people make irrational financial decisions. As per Martin Sewell (2001) Behavioral finance is the study of the influence of psychology on the behavior of financial practitioners and the subsequent effect on markets. Behavioral finance is of interest because it helps explain why and how markets might be inefficient. The field of behavioral finance provides several overarching constructs that elucidate investment performance: it describes the behavior of investors and managers; it describes the outcomes of interactions among investors and managers in financial and capital markets; and it prescribes more effective behavior for investors and managers. In late 1950s and early 1960s Merton Miller and Franco Modigliani described investors as rational in 1961. Eugene Fama described markets as efficient in 1965. Harry Markowitz prescribed

Mean-Variance Portfolio Theory in its early form in 1952 and in its full form in 1959. William Sharpe adopted Mean-Variance Portfolio Theory as a description of investor behavior and in 1964 introduced the Capital Asset Pricing Theory. According to this theory, differences in expected returns are determined only by differences in risk, and beta is the measure of risk. Meir Statman Behavioral finance offers an alternative concept for each of the foundation blocks of standard finance. According to behavioral finance, investors are "normal," not rational. Markets are not efficient, even if they're difficult to beat. Investors design portfolios according to the rules of Behavioral Portfolio Theory, not Mean-Variance Portfolio Theory. And expected returns follow Behavioral Asset Pricing Theory, in which risk is not measured by beta and expected returns are determined by more than risk. When people think about standard finance, they usually think about the Capital Asset Pricing Model and Mean-Variance Portfolio Theory. These two models are elegant, but no one uses them. The elegant Capital Asset Pricing Model has been replaced as standard finance's asset pricing model by the messy three-factor model, which claims that the expected return is not really a function of beta but of market capitalization and the ratio of book value to market value. In turn, the three-factor model has become the four-factor model with the addition of momentum and the five-factor model with the addition of liquidity. The list is likely to grow. Similarly, the mean-variance optimizer is an elegant charade. Quoting Amos Tversky, "Elegance is for tailors." We don't need elegant models; we need models that describe real people in real markets. These are the models of behavioral finance. Behavioral finance offers Behavioral Asset Pricing Theory and Behavioral Portfolio Theory, which are no less elegant than the models of standard finance and are much closer to reality.

Over the past decade, the field of behavioral finance has evolved to consider how personal and social psychology influence financial decisions and the behavior of the financial markets. In 2002, Nobel prize in Economics was given to Daniel Kahneman which highlighted this area for financial practitioners. Now the mainstream financial economists realize that investors can behave irrationally. The paper covers some key aspects of Behavioral Finance and Investor's biases which are discussed in detail as below.

2. PROSPECTS THEORY

In 1979, Daniel Kahneman and Amos Tversky presented an idea called prospect theory which contends that people value gains and losses differently, and, as such, will base decisions on perceived gains rather than perceived losses.

FIGURE 1

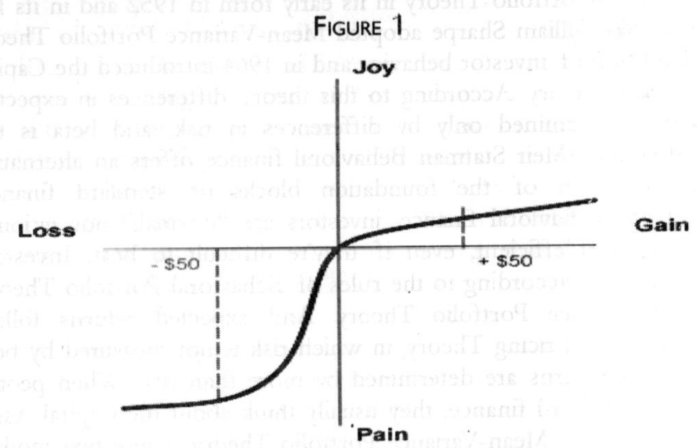

According to prospect theory, losses have more emotional impact than an equivalent amount of gains. Kahneman and Tversky describe how people make decisions through prospect theory as it describes the way people often frame and value decisions involving financial uncertainty. In many situations, investors tend to frame investment choices in terms of potential gains and losses relative to specific reference points. It has been observed that out of so many reference points the original purchase price is the most crucial one which anchors the investment decision of an investor. For example, in a traditional way of thinking, the amount of utility gained from receiving $50 should be equal to a situation in which you gained $100 and then lost $50. In both situations, the end result is a net gain of $50. However, despite the fact that you still end up with a $50 gain in either case, most people view a single gain of $50 more favorably than gaining $100 and then losing $50. Prospect theory also explains the occurrence of the disposition effect, which is the tendency for investors to hold on to losing stocks for too long and sell winning stocks too soon. Investors are willing to assume a higher level of risk in order to avoid the negative utility of a prospective loss. Unfortunately, many of the losing stocks never recover, and the losses incurred continued to mount, with often disastrous results. Therefore, it is said that a skillful investor minimizes investment mistakes so that on-target selections can grow and flourish.

3. ANCHORING AND ADJUSTMENT BIAS

Anchoring and Adjustment is a psychological heuristic that influences the way people intuit probabilities. Investors exhibiting this bias are often influenced by purchase points or arbitrary price levels or price indexes and then tend to cling to these numbers when facing questions like, "Should I buy or sell this security?" or "Is the market overvalued or undervalued right now?". The concept of anchoring draws on the tendency to attach or "anchor" our thoughts to a reference point—even though it may have no logical relevance to the decision at hand. Although it may seem an unlikely phenomenon, anchoring is fairly prevalent in situations where people are dealing with concepts that are new and novel. Some investors invest in the stocks of companies that have fallen considerably in a very short amount of time. In this case, the investor is anchoring on a recent "high" that the stock has achieved and consequently believes that the drop in price provides an opportunity to buy the stock at a discount. Thus, anchoring bias places undue emphasis on statistically arbitrary, psychologically determined anchor points leading to decision-making which deviates from rationality.

3.1 Anchoring Implications

1. Investors tend to make general market forecasts that are too close to current levels. For example, if Sensex is currently at 17500, then the investor will likely to forecast the market between 17000 to 18000 at the end of the year which may not be consistent with the historical standard deviation analysis.
2. Investors and security analysts tend to stick too closely to their original estimates that even when new information is learned about the company the investor doesn't readjusts its asset allocation process in future.
3. Investors tend to make a forecast of the percentage that a particular asset class might rise or fall based on the current level of returns. For example if Sensex provided 80% returns in 2009 then investors will anchor this return while making a forecast in the next year.
4. Investors can become anchored on the economic status of certain countries or companies. For example massive investments in IT companies in late 1990s, which further led to 'bubble' burst.

3.2 Investment Strategies—Anchoring and Adjustment Biases

An awareness of the mechanics of anchoring and adjustment bias can actually serve as a fundamental tenet of a successful investment strategy. If an analyst is anchored to an earnings estimate and earnings are rising, then this is an opportunity for investors to win, as it is likely that the analyst is underestimating the magnitude of the earnings upgrades. Similarly, when earnings are falling, it's the best time to sell immediately on the first downgrade, as it is likely that the analyst is underestimating the magnitude of the earnings downgrades.

4. MENTAL ACCOUNTING AND FRAMING BIAS

Mental accounting was first coined by Richard Thaler, Professor of Finance, University of Chicago. It describes people's tendency to code, categorize and evaluate economic outcomes by grouping their assets into any number of non-interchangeable mental accounts based on a variety of subjective criteria, like the source of the money and intent for each account. According to the theory, individuals assign different functions to each asset group, which has an often irrational and detrimental effect on their consumption decisions and other behaviors. The Behavioral Portfolios pyramid of the mental accounts can be illustrated as below:

1. *Wealth preserving investments*: CDs, money market, mutual funds, T-bills, life insurance, home insurance, etc.
2. *Wealth building investments*: Treasury bonds, investment grade corporate bonds, broad market index funds, high yield common stocks, etc.
3. *Aggressive wealth building investments*: Individual common stocks, small cap index funds, foreign stocks, etc.
4. *Speculation*: IPOs, market timings, tech stocks, short selling, junk bonds, etc.
5. *Funny money*: Lotto tickets, casino gambling, day trading, etc.

Behavioral portfolios are not necessarily designed from the standpoint of minimizing risk and maximizing expected return through optimal diversification across asset categories. Instead they are determined by the distribution of investment goal and associated mental accounts thus from an economic perspective, this means that many investors end up taking on more risk than necessary for the level of expected return they are getting.

4.1 Mental Accounting Implications

1. Mental accounting bias can cause people to imagine that their investments occupy separate buckets or accounts that correspond with specified financial goals leading to sub-optimal portfolio performance.
2. Mental accounting bias treats returns of income and capital appreciations irrationally, i.e. people feel the need to preserve capital and prefers to spend the interest. As a result, investors may chase income streams and can unwittingly erode principal in the process.

3. Mental accounting bias can cause investors to escalate risk-taking behaviors as wealth grows. Investors endanger their portfolios while exhibiting this irrationality because they fail to treat all money as fungible.
4. Mental accounting bias can cause investors to hesitate to sell investments that once generated significant gains but overtime have fallen in price.

4.2 Investment Strategies—Mental Accounting and Framing Bias

It is important for financial practitioners to recognize that mental accounting can sometimes generate benefits provided they adhere to "goal-based planning" and set multiple, distinctive goals for their clients. Since it is difficult to reconcile single portfolio framework with the existence of separate mental accounts linked with specific investment goals but still 'goal-based investing' could be implemented which manages the risk of not achieving goal rather than relying on traditional risk measures.

5. CONFIRMATION AND HINDSIGHT BIAS

(A) *Confirmation Bias*: It is based on a preconceived opinion of investor which tends to skew an investor's frame of reference, leaving them with an incomplete picture of the situation. People also tend to selectively filter and pay more attention to information that supports their opinions, while ignoring or rationalizing the rest that might discount their claims.

5.1 Investment Strategies—Confirmation Bias

1. The first step towards eliminating the bias is that to confirm that the bias exists. It is important to understand that mere existence of contradictory evidence does not necessarily mean an investment was unwise. Even the most precisely calculated judgement can go away.
2. When investment is based on some preexisting criteria like trend of 52 week highs, then it is advisable to verify the decision from additional angles to overcome preconceived notions.
3. Over concentrating in company stock (ESOPs) is inadvisable for numerous reasons. Employees must monitor any negative press regarding their own company and conduct research on any competing firms.

4. Overconcentration in a single company is also detrimental since the clients do not want to hear anything negative about favored investments like in case of investments in Reliance Industries especially the IPO of reliance power. These kinds of behavior results into lopsided portfolios.

(B) *Hindsight Bias*: It tends to occur in situations where a person believes (after_the fact) that the onset of some past event was predictable and completely obvious, whereas in fact, the event could not have been reasonably predicted. In this case, overconfidence refers to investors' or traders' unfounded belief that they possess superior stock-picking abilities. One detriment of hindsight bias is that it can prevent learning from mistakes and find it difficult to reconstruct the unbiased state of mind. In sum, hindsight bias leads people to exaggerate the quality of their forecasts.

5.2 Investment Strategies—Hindsight Bias

1. Encouragement to self-examination of past all investment decision—both good and bad can provide insights and learn from the past investment mistakes to find investment success.
2. Investors should not unduly criticize money managers for unduly poor performance since markets move in cycles and at certain times investment managers do underperform their own class relative to other asset classes. In January 2007 when all stocks were underperforming then that doesn't mean that growth managers were unskilled.
3. In financial markets there are plenty of investment managers who have over performed from market returns but that doesn't mean they will continue to perform this always. This provides clear indication for an investor to continuously monitor the fund manager to curtail the hindsight bias.

6. OVERCONFIDENCE BIAS

Overconfidence is unwarranted faith in one's intuitive reasoning, judgments, and cognitive abilities. In short, people think they are smarter and have better information than they actually do. Both prediction and certainty overconfidence can lead to making investment mistakes and can cause harm to an investor's portfolio.

In a 2006 study entitled "Behaving Badly", researcher James Montier found that 74% of the 300 professional fund managers surveyed believed that they had delivered above-average job performance. Of the remaining 26% surveyed, the majority viewed themselves as average. Incredibly, almost 100% of the survey group believed that their job performance was average or better. Clearly, only 50% of the sample can be above average, suggesting the irrationally high level of overconfidence these fund managers exhibited in the study.

6.1 Overconfident Investing

In a 1998 study entitled "Volume, Volatility, Price, and Profit When All Traders Are above Average", researcher Terrence Odean found that overconfident investors generally conduct more trades than their less-confident counterparts. Odean found that overconfident investors/traders tend to believe they are better than others at choosing the best stocks and the best times to enter/exit a position. Unfortunately, Odean also found that traders that conducted the most trades tended, on average, to receive significantly lower yields than the market.

7. AVAILABILITY BIAS

The availability bias is a rule of thumb, or mental shortcut, that allows people to estimate the probability of an outcome based on how prevalent or familiar that outcome appears in their lives. Under this bias the investors ignore potentially beneficial investments because information on those investments is not available and avoiding diligent research. The effects of availability bias on portfolio management are discussed as follows:

1. *Retrievability*: Investors will choose investments based on information that is available to them (advertising, suggestions from advisors, friends, etc.) and will not engage in disciplined research or due diligence to verify that the investment selected is a good one.
2. *Categorisation*: Investors will select only those investments which are available in their memories and ignore those which are not easily called whether they are potentially rewarding investment opportunities.
3. *Narrow range of experience*: Investors will choose investments that fit a narrow range of life experiences, such as the industry they work in, the region they live in, and the people they associate with.
4. *Resonance*: Investors will choose investments that resonate with their own personality or that have characteristics that

investor can relate to their own behavior. For example, a thrifty individual who discounts shops, clips coupons and otherwise seeks out bargains may demonstrate a natural inclination towards value investing and may not relate to expensive stocks thus missing out to the benefits of owing these stocks.

8. OVERREACTION

In 1985, behavioral finance academics Werner De Bondt and Richard Thaler released a study in the *Journal of Finance* called "Does the Market Overreact?" In this study, the two examined returns on the New York Stock Exchange for a three-year period. From these stocks, they separated the best 35 performing stocks into a "winners portfolio" and the worst 35 performing stocks were then added to a "losers portfolio". De Bondt and Thaler then tracked each portfolio's performance against a representative market index for three years. Does stock market overreacts De Bondt Thaler (1985). Surprisingly, it was found that the losers portfolio consistently beat the market index, while the winners portfolio consistently underperformed. In total, the cumulative difference between the two portfolios was almost 25% during the three-year time span. In other words, it appears that the original "winners" would became "losers", and *vice versa.*

FIGURE 2

Cumulative Average Residuals for Winner and Loser Portfolio of 35 Stocks (1-36 months into the test period)

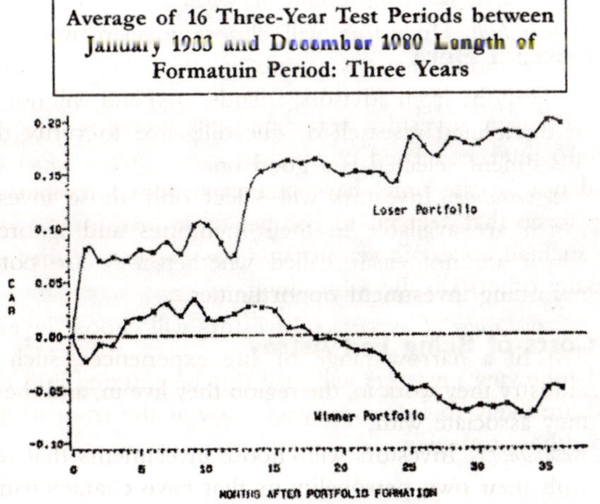

9. GAMBLER'S FALLACY

When it comes to probability, a lack of understanding can lead to incorrect assumptions and predictions about the onset of events. One of these incorrect assumptions is called the gambler's fallacy. In the gambler's fallacy, an individual erroneously believes that the onset of a certain random event is less likely to happen following an event or a series of events. This line of thinking is incorrect because past events do not change the probability that certain events will occur in the future.

9.1 Gambler's Fallacy in Investing

Some investors believe that they should liquidate a position after it has gone up in a series of subsequent trading sessions because they don't believe that the position is likely to continue going up. Conversely, other investors might hold on to a stock that has fallen in multiple sessions because they view further declines as "improbable". Just because a stock has gone up on six consecutive trading sessions does not mean that it is less likely to go up on during the next session.

10. HERD BEHAVIOR

Herd Behavior is a tendency for individuals to mimic the actions (rational or irrational) of a larger group. Individually, however, most people would not necessarily make the same choice. There are two reasons for Herd Behavior:

1. Social pressure of conformity.
2. Second reason is the common rationale that it's unlikely that such a large group could be wrong.

10.1 The Dotcom Herd

Herd behavior was exhibited in the late 1990s as venture capitalists and private investors were frantically investing huge amounts of money into internet-related companies, even though most of these dotcoms did not (at the time) have financially sound business models. The driving force that seemed to compel these investors to sink their money into such an uncertain venture was the reassurance they got from seeing so many others do the same thing.

10.2 The Costs of Being Led Astray

Herd-following investors will probably be entering into the game too late and are likely to lose money as those at the front of the pack move on to other strategies.

11. SUMMARY AND CONCLUDING REMARKS

There is a paradigm shift of attention from Efficient Market Hypothesis to Behavioral Finance. Even though there is no concrete set of theory or a model of investor behavior but still a lot can be understood by identifying various investment biases experienced by investors (individual of institutional) and develop rational portfolios. The main lesson from the above discussion is that theory doesn't tell people how to beat the market but how psychology causes market prices and fundamental values to diverge for a long time. The discipline of behavioral finance can help successful investors to monitor their progress towards their financial goals and make necessary asset allocation adjustments through periodic portfolio rebalancing.

References

Sewell, M., (2008), "Behavioral Finance", Department of Computer Science, University College, London, www.behavioralfinance.net/

Statman, Meir, "A behavioral framework for dollar-cost averaging", *Journal of Portfolio Management*, Vol. 22 (Fall. 1995).

Kahneman, Daniel and Amos Tversky, Prospect Theory: An Analysis of Decision under Risk, *Econometrica*, Volume 47, Issue 2 (Mar., 1979), 263-292.

Tversky, Amos and Daniel Kahneman (1986), Rational Choice and the Framing of Decisions, *Journal of Business*, Volume 59, Issue 4, Part 2: The Behavioral Foundations of Economic Theory (Oct., 1986), S251-S278.

Kahneman, Daniel and Amos Tversky (Jan. 30, 1981), "Judgement under Uncertainty: Heuristics and Biases", *Science*, New Series, Volume 185, Issue 4157, pp 1124-31.

Shefrin, H. (2007), "Individual Investors", Beyond Greed and Fear: Understanding Behavioral Finance and the Psychology of Investing, Financial Management Association Survey and Synthesis Series, Oxford University Press, New York, pp. 107-19.

Pompian, M. Micheal (2006), "Investors' Biases defined and illustrated", Behavioral Finance and Wealth Management, John Wiley & Sons, Inc., Hooboken, New Jersey, USA, pp. 51-199.

Jaffe, W.R. (2004), "Corporate financing decisions and Efficient capital markets", Corporate Finance, Tata McGraw Hills, Seventh Edition, New Delhi, pp. 364-65.

Odean, Terrence (1998), "Volume, Volatility, Price, and Profit When All Traders Are above Average", *Journal of Finance*, 53, 1775-98.

De Bondt, Werner F.M. and Richard Thaler (1985), Does the Stock Market Overreact?, *Journal of Finance*, Volume 40, Issue 3, Papers and Proceedings of the Forty-third Annual Meeting, American Finance Association, Dallas, Texas, December 28-30, 1984 (Jul., 1985), 793-805.

Bodie, Z., Kane, A., Marcus, A. and Pitabas Mohanty (2007), "Market Efficiency and Behavioral Finance", Investments, Tata McGraw Hills, Third Edition, New Delhi, pp. 404-08.

Hirschey, M., John Nofsinger (2008), "Psychology and the Stock Market", Investments—Analysis and Behavior, Tata McGraw Hills, First Edition, New Delhi, pp. 209-34.

Ofek, E. and M. Richardson (2003), "Dot-com mania: market inefficiency in the internet sector", *Journal of Finance*, 58: 1113-37.

Brealy, A.R., Stewart C. Mayers, Franklin Allen and Mohanty (2007), "Financing Decisions and Market Efficiency", Principles of Corporate Finance, Tata McGraw Hills, Second Edition, New Delhi, pp. 350-57.

Websites used

www.investopaedia.com
www.behavioralfinance.net
http://online.wsj.com
www.wileyfinance.com
www.fpanet.com
www.iijournals.com
www.businessstandard.com

14

Banking and Finance Sector Crisis: Strategic Dimensions and Directions in the Era of Economic Meltdown

Roshni Mohanty and Sasikanta Tripathy

INTRODUCTION

This is one of the most challenging phases our economy has seen in a very long time, especially when it comes fast on the back of what has been the golden era of the Indian economy. With the economic slowdown and its impact on various sectors, both the RBI and the Central Government are trying their best to infuse liquidity and give a stimulus to the economy. They have diluted norms so that companies and businesses facing problems are given certain relaxations in terms of prudential norms and asset classification and a chance to restructure their loans. Thousands of institutions in micro, tiny, medium and large industries, and several export units, have been affected by the current slowdown in the economy. Wherever the advances are restructured in such cases, the banks have been permitted to classify them as standard assets. You have to judge whether the loan has been restructured because there is a genuine problem, or if the bank is trying to keep it as a standard asset although it is a non-performing asset. New generation banks have created a niche for itself as a 'knowledge-driven

Organisation'. The aim is to be a simple, high-tech Indian banks catering to industries which have a growth potential. The challenges are across the board. On our asset side, banks are roughly 60 per cent wholesale banking, 30 per cent commercial banking and 6-7 per cent SME banking. The consumer loan book is less than 1 per cent. The maximum impact has been on consumer loans. The consumer loan portfolio has been adversely impacted across the industry. Banks were running a pilot about 18 months ago and they consciously decelerated our consumer portfolio. Banks saw heightened pricing, risk appetite in the market and we consciously slowed down that business. That portfolio is Rs. 15 crore. Banks are running it down, as and when payments come. It is too small in relation to the banks balance sheet, which is almost Rs. 22,000 crore and its loan book is Rs. 12,500 crore. SME is well collateralised in our case. There is some manageable delay in just one or two accounts. In the corporate portfolio, whether it is commercial or wholesale banking, there is concern in industries such as retail, textile and automobiles.

The Bank is marching into next century position as an institution offering the best of two worlds with a sound heritage and foundation and committed staff with a new-age attitude and drive. Banks provide superior, pro-active, innovative state-of-the-art banking services with an attitude of care and concern for the customers and patrons. Our strength is our brand image and customer loyalty. This will be the basic genesis on which we would like to leverage business growth. Public sector banks in India are sound and safe as they don't want to show anything which is not true, according to Mr. J.M. Garg, Chairman and Managing Director of Corporation Bank.

Objectives

This study takes a closer look at the counter strategies taken by Banks at the times of Crisis and Economic Meltdown. It focuses on how Banks inspite of the crisis have placed themselves at win-win situation.

Banking Sector

Banks will move towards customer acquisitions more innovatively. Banks will have to be more transparent with products, services, prices. And banks will have to continuously explore ways to augment capital and, more importantly, preserve it. It is found to be sobering that these themes continue to be important. With financial inclusion being pushed at by banks and the Government due to a happy mix of reasons business expanding beyond Tier-1 and 2 cities and fetching a new set of customers, and inclusive growth that brings unbanked areas into the banking fold — financial literacy becomes imperative. They see deposits growing by 35-40 per cent, which will be a combination of retail, small, medium and large businesses. On the loan side, a loan book growth of around 25 per cent for the next one year is a more reasonable target. Banks would have aspired to do more, but right now they also need to be cautious. Banks need to grow in some segments and also grow in some others. It will have to churn some our assets; sell down or get repayment in industries impacted by the global onslaught. Cost of funds has been moving up and down. They are still at levels of 9.4-9.5 per cent. But the Net Interest Margin has been holding up. In the October-December period, the NIM was stable at 2.8 per cent. Banks believe they can improve it in a declining interest rate scenario. Banks will be happy if they stabilise around 3 per cent. For 2012, banks target is to get to 25 per cent CASA. At that level they should be looking at NIMs of 3.5 per cent. By 2015 banks should stabilise NIM at around 3.75 per cent and 30 per cent CASA.

STRATEGIES

Capital Investments

Banks have beefed up our Tier I with our maiden hybrid Tier I issue. The issue size was Rs. 75 crore and we mobilised Rs. 150 crore. This is a perpetual debt issue. Banks were paying 10.25 per cent on an annualised basis. It's mainly public sector banks that have invested. In 2008-09, through a combination of hybrid Tier I, retail earnings and upper Tier II capital, they would have accreted a minimum of Rs. 1,000 crore in 2008-09, from an approximate base of less than Rs. 2,000 crore at the beginning of the fiscal. They have not raised any lower Tier II capital this year. With this our capital funds will be in excess of Rs. 3,000 crore. Their capital adequacy will be in excess of 15 per cent. This capital is good enough for us till June 2010. In the first half of next fiscal, we will target Rs. 400-450 crore of lower Tier II capital, which will do till September 2010 at a loan growth rate of 25 per cent. In 2009-10, we may go through some minor changes. Banks may probably see 45 per cent contribution from non-interest income and 55 per cent from interest income.

Retail Banking

Banks had periods of fairly high financial market activity and financial advisory activity. But there is some balance now, because our transaction banking activity has stepped up. The activities in retail on the back of account opening, remittances, payments, insurance and mutual funds sales have stepped up. In the current environment, two important factors come into play — slowdown in growth and falling inflation. Both these factors are conducive enough for interest rates to move southwards. The RBI will have to cut interest rates to get the economy back on a growth trajectory. Lower interest rates would encourage consumer spending and corporate investments, which would bolster the economy. Inflation is expected to slide down below 3 per cent by the end of March 2009, which would give the RBI more leeway to cut interest rates. Commercial Banks expect the Central Bank to cut the reverse repo rate and the repo rates. In the last few months, risk aversion has increased considerably, capital availability has reduced drastically and liquidity has tightened significantly. All these factors have led to widening of corporate spreads and a resultant increase in the cost of borrowing for corporates. Therefore, in spite of huge rate cuts by the RBI, interest burden remains high for the corporates.

Corporate Credit Spreads

Credit is now extended with more caution than before. Here is the rub: none of them (0) said there was a particular problem with trade credit. The general view was that until recent times were so good that everyone received credit without loan officers having to look carefully at the company's income flows. Now there is increased vigilance. But that vigilance extends to the overall health of the business, and is not specific to companies dependent on international trade. Of course, if global demand for particular goods has fallen, with an associated collapse in prices, bankers will get worried. And as export prices for many goods has fallen by 30-60%, there is enough reason to worry indeed. This said, the main issue is falling demand, not lack of credit. It could be that international organizations understand this (they have enough good economists) but think donors are more likely to fork out extra cash if the "international trading system is at risk." And it could be that this is a good strategy as it gives some businesses in emerging markets extra room to maneuver during the economic downturn. So all is good, except if the new credits are really focused on international trade, despite the obvious lack of demand. That could finance excess capacity in the coming months, and further depress prices. Fortunately, businesses, not bureaucrats, will in the end decide how to use the money. And they probably realize by now that the domestic market may be where they can focus the attention, and wait for demand in OECD countries to pick up.

Currently, the credit spreads of Indian corporates are at an all-time high. As explained, the availability of funds, even for highly rated companies, is tough in the current environment. Unless we witness return of risk appetite among the investors which, in our opinion, will take some time, corporates will find it difficult to raise funds despite ECB relaxation. The 10-year gilt had bottomed at 5 per cent and gone up later, hurting bond prices. Then gains in gilt investment going to be difficult from here on. The month of January has been very volatile for government bond markets. The reversal was essentially on account of an additional borrowing programme announced by the government. With 3G auction now being suspect, there is a further possibility of additional borrowing. This uncertainty over borrowing in a short time-frame is causing volatility. Once the negative news is absorbed, there is a very high probability that the yields of government bonds will fall further due to expected rate cuts by the RBI. Banks would like to reiterate the fact that we expect the RBI to cut rates further to limit the downside risk to growth. In the opinion, the probability of growth coming below 7 per cent is very high. Global slowdown and uncertainties, falling exports and slowdown in consumption might bring down growth below this level. On the inflation front, we expect it to be below 3 per cent and even getting in the negative zone in the first quarter of 2009-10. We expect a host of data on the industry side to be negative in the coming months. Therefore, giving the current background and expectations of a soft interest rate regime, we have increased the duration of the portfolio. This would help banks to take maximum advantage of falling yields. Currently, the credit spreads of the corporates are at an all-time high and do make an attractive investment option. However, corporate bonds currently carry relative liquidity risk. In addition, the current economic background warrants caution thus making us more selective on the choice of credit. Therefore, one will have to strike a balance between good quality corporate portfolio and gilts. As such, banks are currently restricting our investments to high quality liquid PSU/quasi-sovereign debt papers.

Reduction in NPA's

Though the interest rate movements resulted in an increase in cost of deposits, strategies like concentration on high yielding advances, faster recycling of funds through short-term loans at competitive rates, reduction in NPAs, etc. all lead to an increase in yield on advances. As a result, the net impact on NIM was considerably contained. The Banks strategy of concentrating on recoveries in written-off accounts, commission income from government business and referral income from distribution of third party products, etc. also yielded good results. I am very happy to announce that as a result of all these efforts, your bank has posted a handsome increase in net profit by 78.50% over the previous year, i.e. from Rs. 201.56 crore to Rs. 359.79 crore. A dividend at the rate of 10% as against 8% for the previous year has been recommended by the Board, considering need of higher ploughback of profits to augment capital funds to support growth of assets at higher rate in view of the limiting factors in accessing further Equity by the Bank.

Liberalized Credit for SSI

Banks extend production-linked credit facilities to small-scale industries, ancillary industrial units and village and cottage industrial units on liberal terms and conditions. Under this scheme, the quantum of advances is not linked to the security furnished, but the genuine requirements of the unit. The pricing of the loan is based on credit assessment, and the units with strong ratings may be given finer rates. No collateral security is required for loans up to Rs. 5 lakh. Composite term loans can be sanctioned up to Rs. 25 lakh combining term loan and working capital.

The Liberalized scheme offers a range of financial products including the following:

1. Term loans for acquisition of fixed assets.
2. Working capital loans financing current assets.
3. Letter of credit for acquisition of machinery and purchase of raw materials.
4. Bank guarantee in lieu of security deposits to be made with government department/other departments for execution of orders.
5. Deferred payment guarantees for the purchase of machinery on deferred payment basis.
6. Bill facility for purchase of raw materials and for sale of finished goods.
7. Composite loans (term loans plus working capital) up to Rs. 25 lakh.

Entrepreneur Scheme

Bank grant financial assistance to technically qualified, trained and experienced entrepreneurs for setting up new viable industrial projects. Loans are extended to technocrats who are unable to meet the normal margin requirements under the liberalized schemes. The borrower has to be a technically qualified person (a degree/diploma holder in engineering or technology), a craftsman with adequate experience or training or a person possessing a degree in business or industrial management, a chartered accountant or a cost accountant with relevant experience. The bank provides term loans, working capital and equity fund finance. For requirements upto Rs. 5 lakh, no margins are involved. For needs ranging from Rs. 5 lakh to Rs. 20 lakh, the margin is set at 10 per cent.

CONCLUSION

The recent financial tsunami that has relegated many a 'successful' bank to the bins of history, compelled governments to step in to recapitalise many of them, and raised soul-searching questions about risk management, leaving in its wake more answers than questions.

REFERENCES

Bayoumi, T., and Mauro, P. (1999), The Suitability of ASEAN for a Regional Currency Arrangement, *IMF Working Paper*, 99-162.

Bergsten, C.F. (1997), The Asian Monetary Crisis: Proposed Remedies, Testimony before the Committee on Banking and Financial Services, US House of Representatives, Institute for International Economics, 7-19.

DeMarzo, P., Kaniel, R., and Kremer, I. (2007), Technological innovation and real investment booms and busts, *Journal of Financial Economics*, 85, 735-54.

Evrensel, A.Y. (2008), Banking crisis and financial structure: A survival-time analysis, *International Review of Economics and Finance*, 17, 589-602.

Guo, F., Chen, C.R., and Huang, Y.S. (2011), Markets contagion during financial crisis: A regime switching approach, *International Review of Economics and Finance*, 20, 95-109.

Kaminsky, G.L., and Reinhart, C.M. (1999), The twin crisis: The causes of banking and balance-of-payments problems, *The American Economic Review*, 89(3), 473-500.

Laeven, L., Igan, D., and Dell'Ariccia, G. (2008), Credit booms and lending standards: Evidence from the subprime mortgage market, *IMF Working Paper*, 8-106.

Roy, S., and Kemme, D.M. (2011), What is really common in the run-up to banking crises? *Economics Letters*, 113, 211-14.

Transforming Banking through Tech-Driven Mobility

DR. SAJAN MATHEW AND DR. RAY TITUS

INTRODUCTION

The technology throughout the globe is on a rapid development. This know-how extravaganza has hit the banking sector. With the advancements in m-commerce, banking services are made available to the customers with the use of their mobile gadgets. High-tech gurus of the banking world are spending a lot of time these days dreaming of the bank of the future. If things go as some techies predict, the bank branch of the future will likely be customers' own living rooms.

Research Methodology

This research initiative prompts a look at Mobile Banking and its practice. It first focuses on contemporary trends that are in practice in the Mobile Banking Arena. It explores these practices both from a process perspective and in terms of the technologies that are at play. The research work also navigates the service value propositions that are being built for the consumer through the use of mobile banking. Finally, it proposes a technology services model that can pave for the future of mobile banking. The proposed futuristic model (Banking Information Systems model) optimizes of value enhancement for the two key stakeholders in the mobile engagement, namely, the banking institution, and the service user (customer).

The Advent and Use of Mobile Banking

Mobile banking (also known as M-Banking, m-banking, SMS Banking, etc.) is a term used for performing balance checks, account transactions, payments, etc. via a mobile device such as a mobile phone. Mobile banking is an obvious extension of online banking as cell phones get more powerful and begin to mimic computers. Mobile banking today (2007) is most often performed via *SMS* or the *Mobile Internet* but can also use special programs downloaded to the mobile device. The trend of Mobile Banking is on a rise because some of the largest U.S. banks —Bank of America, Citibank, Wachovia, Washington Mutual, Wells Fargo, and ING Direct—are launching mobile banking services that give you access to your accounts wherever you are. Though still in its infancy, these banks are hoping the mobile service will catch on with consumers.

FIGURE 1

Bank of America and CitiBank Mobile Bank Portals

If we see the future of banking every mobile phone company has an opportunity to become a big bank and all banking companies should be afraid of mobile devices. Presently, everyone has a credit card and these credit cards use RFID technology but now these technologies are also available on mobile phones and that's the most interesting part.

Imagine in the future if people want to make payment for school fees, at the station, at restaurants or any place for that matter then instead of going to the bank for making payments an SMS will come to their mobile and then they will just need to put their thumb on the screen so that the device knows who the person is and that person can simply press pay button to make the payment.

Suppose that a son who wants to send money back home then he can simply have two copies of a SIM, one he can own and one he can give it to his father, then he can simply buy minutes on his mobile phone and his father can use that money back home and can spend it the way his father wants. He can buy a car or can trade it the way he wants. This facility is presently provided by Vodafone in some countries. The major advantage of it is that there is no foreign exchange transaction, no banking losses, no control and most importantly no taxes.

The idea behind the bank of tomorrow is to have a more relaxing and inviting experience with the bank. This will be accomplished through innovative technology and digitization. The bank of future will be one in which if a customer picks up a brochure of car insurance, relevant information would flash up on the plasma screen and alert staff to a customer's interest in the product.

MOBILE BANKING SERVICES

Mobile banking can offer a variety of services such as the following:

1. Mini-statements and checking of account history.
2. Alerts on account activity or passing of set thresholds, etc.
3. Domestic and international fund transfers.
4. Micro-payment handling, etc.
5. Portfolio management services.
6. Real-time stock quotes.
7. General information such as weather updates, news, etc.

FIGURE 2

Most Common Mobile Banking Functions

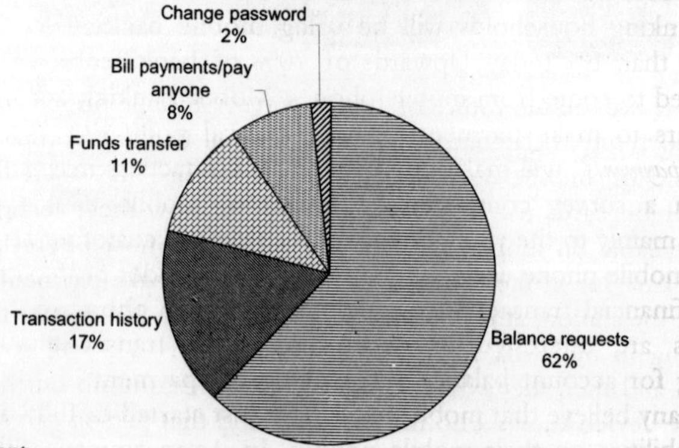

Source: Celent.

The following Figure 3 shows the mobile banking regional forecast by Jupiter research.

FIGURE 3

Mobile Banking Regional Forecast

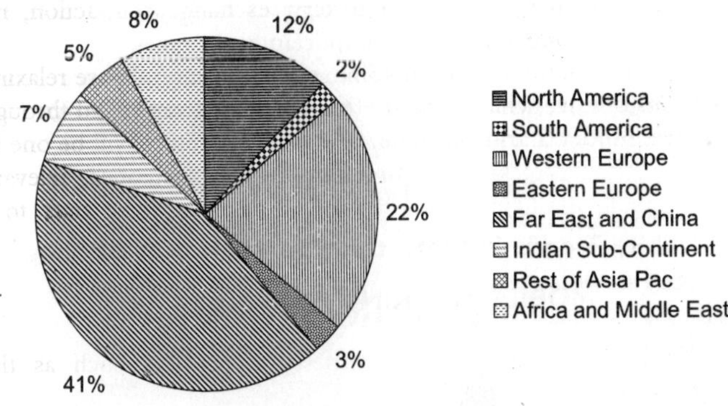

juniper-research-mobile-banking-transactional-users-global

LATEST TRENDS IN MOBILE BANKING

Over the last few years, the mobile and wireless market has been one of the fastest growing markets in the world and it is still growing at a rapid pace. According to the GSM Association and Ovum, the number of mobile subscribers exceeded 2 billion in September 2005, and now exceeds 2.5 billion (of which more than 2 billion are GSM).

According to a study by financial consultancy *Celent*, 35% of online banking households will be using mobile banking by 2011, up from less than 1% today. Upwards of 70% of bank center call volume is projected to come from mobile phones. Mobile banking will eventually allow users to make payments at the physical point of sale. "Mobile *contactless payments*" will make up 10% of the contactless market by 2011. Based on a survey conducted by Forrester, mobile banking will be attractive mainly to the younger, more "tech-savvy" customer segment. A third of mobile phone users say that they may consider performing some kind of financial transaction through their mobile phone. But most of the users are interested in performing basic transactions such as querrying for account balance and making bill payment.

Many believe that mobile users have just started to fully utilize the data capabilities on their mobile phones. In Asian countries like India,

China, Indonesia and Philippines, where mobile infrastructure is comparatively better than the fixed-line infrastructure, and in European countries, where mobile phone penetration is very high (at least 80% of consumers use a mobile phone), mobile banking is likely to appeal even more. The proliferation of the 3G (third generation of wireless) and widespread implementation expected in future will generate the development of more sophisticated services such as multimedia and links to m-commerce services.

Presently some smart banks are already using intelligent cameras to track customers' behavior in the branches in order to provide more customized products and services.

FIGURE 4

Mobile Trends Indicate the Potential of m-Banking

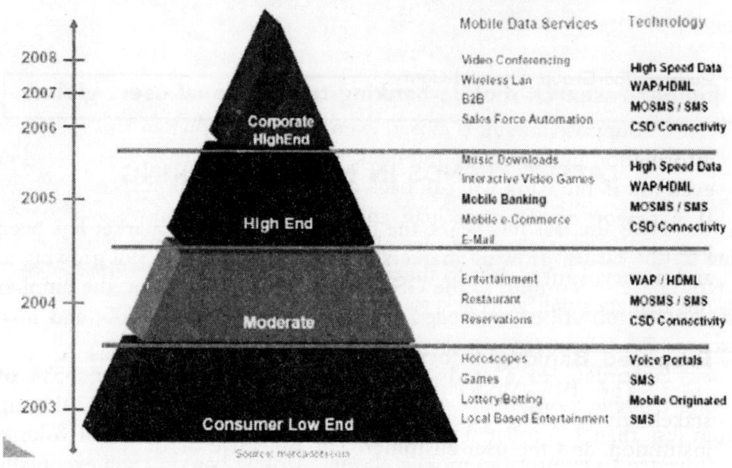

In the future even if a person is near a bank and not inside then he can with the help of mobile phones that acts as a virtual bank card can interact with banks this happens because of what is known as **Location-based services** in which the functions is acquired based on the location in which the person is. If he is in a super market it becomes a store card and tells about the special offers, deals and discounts and if the person is near a bank it acts as a bank card. With the help of such technology people can interact and transact with the bank by using devices like smart phones even without going to the nearest local branch.

FIGURE 5

Per-transaction Costs by Banking Channels

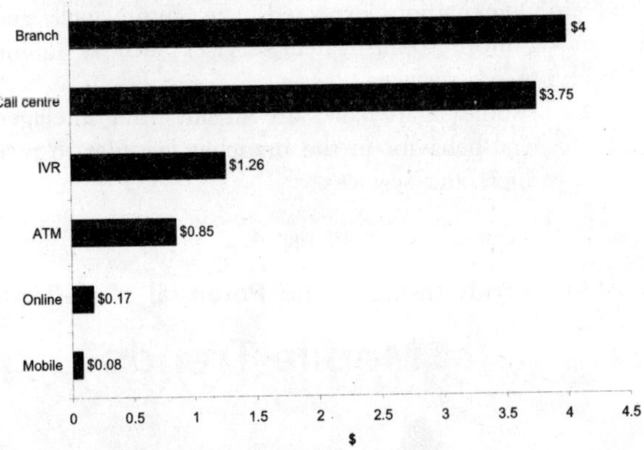

Source: ToerGroup, Fiserv/M-Com.

Suppose a bank is closed even then a person can still get personal information like what are the bank timings, who the manager is and can even ask if the bank will call back and the phone will receive a text back. If a person needs a car loan and they have a phone they can get all perspective to it, they can save all calculations in the phone just by touch and if they want to talk to the manager he can just select that option and the manager will get back to the person.

Proposed Banking Information System (BIS) Model

The BIS Model illustrated on next page engages two key stakeholders through a mobile platform, namely, the banking services institution, and the user-customer. The objective of the flow of mobile-driven information is to enhance on value delivery to the two key stakeholders involved. The Banking institution leverages on the mobility platform to use information better to optimize on marketing its services better to its customer which in turn both locks in, and builds stronger relationship engagement with its customers. The Consumer on his part enjoys greater value through optimized financial services that are customized in its usage.

The usage of the BIS model paves way for a win-win for both banking services and its users. It also ensures that resources are both mobilized and used in a manner ©where there's value enhancement for both the key stakeholders.

FIGURE 6

Proposed Banking Information System (BIS) Model

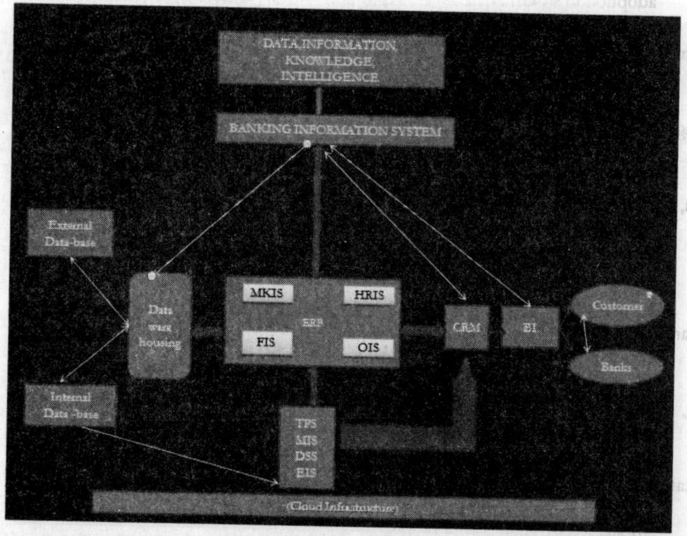

CONCLUSION

Thus the future of banking is here. From withdrawals to loan approvals and payments, everything can be done with a touch or a key on the mobile phones such as PDAs, smart phones and other mobile devices. In future, people will enjoy the banking services like never before. In the near future, the mobile device will slowly morph into a ubiquitous payment device, both for remote and proximity-based point of sale payments throughout the world. By implementing an enterprise-wide mobile financial services platform today, financial institutions will be better positioned to take full advantage of the revenue-generating opportunities that mobile payments will provide.

REFERENCES

Anckar, B., and D. fIncau, D., "Value-Added Services in Mobile Commerce: An Analytical Framework and Empirical Findings from a National Consumer Survey," 35th Hawaii International Conference on Systems Sciences, 2002.

Anderson, J., "M-banking in developing markets: competitive and regulatory implications," Info: *The Journal of Policy, Regulation and Strategy for Telecommunications* (12:1) 2010, pp. 18-25.

Barnes, S.J., and Corbitt, B., "Mobile banking: concept and potential," *International Journal of Mobile Communications* (1:3) 2003, pp 273-288.

Bonina, C.M., and Illa, M.R., "Mobile Telephony in Latin America: New Opportunities to Reduce Poverty?," Americas Conference on Information Systems, 2008, p. 188.

Brown, I., Cajee, Z., Davies, D., and Stroebel, S., "Cell phone banking: predictors of adoption in South Africa—an exploratory study," *International Journal of Information Management* (23:5), Oct. 2003, pp. 381-94.

Brown, I., Gordon, C., Janik, N., and Meyer, M., "Investigating Adoption/Non-Adoption of Cell Phones for Financial Transactions in South Africa," Australasian Conference on Information Systems, 2005, p. 51.

Chang, P.C., and Melbourne, A., "2 Drivers and Moderators of Consumer Behavior in the Multiple Use of Mobile Phone," Australasian Conference on Information Systems, 2008, p. 68.

Chen, Z., Lee, M., and Cheung, C., "A framework for mobile commerce," Americas Conference on IS, 2001.

Chu, S., and Yao-bin, L., "Effect of Online-to-Mobile Trust Transfer and Previous Satisfaction on the Foundation of Mobile Banking Initial Trust," 8th International Conference on Mobile Business, 2009, pp. 1-6.

Suoranta, M., and Mattila, M., "Mobile banking and consumer behavior: New insights into the diffusion pattern," *Journal of Financial Services Marketing* (8:4), 06 2004, pp. 354-66.

Tang, T.I., Lin, H.H., Wang, Y.S., and Wang, Y.M., "Toward An Understanding of the Behavioral Intention to Use Mobile Banking Services," Pacific Asia Conference on Information Systems, 2004, p. 131.

Venkatesh, V., "Where To Go From Here? Thoughts on Future Directions for Research on Individual-Level Technology Adoption with a Focus on Decision-making," *Decision Sciences* (37:4) 2006, pp. 497-518.

Wang, Y.-S., Hsin-Hui, L., and Pin, L., "Predicting consumer intention to use mobile service," *Information Systems Journal* (16:2), 04 2006, pp. 157-79.

Wati, Y., Koo, C., Jung, J., and Li, D., "An Empirical Analysis of End-User Satisfaction toward E-Banking in Indonesia," Americas Conference on IS, 2009, p. 30.

Weber, R.H., and Darbellay, A. "Legal issues in mobile banking," *Journal of Banking Regulation* (11:2) 2010. Wu, J.H., and Wang, S.C., "What drives mobile commerce? An empirical evaluation of the revised technology acceptance model," *Information & Management* (42:5) 2005, pp. 719-29.

Xiangpei, H., Wenli, L., and Qing, H., "Are Mobile Payment and Banking the Killer Apps for Mobile Commerce?," 41st Hawaii International Conference on System Sciences, 2008, ©p. 84.

Index